GREEN MOVEMENT IN BUSINESS

GREEN MOVEMENT IN BUSINESS

KARIN E. SANCHEZ
EDITOR

Nova Science Publishers, Inc.
New York

Copyright © 2009 by Nova Science Publishers, Inc.

All rights reserved. No part of this book may be reproduced, stored in a retrieval system or transmitted in any form or by any means: electronic, electrostatic, magnetic, tape, mechanical photocopying, recording or otherwise without the written permission of the Publisher.

For permission to use material from this book please contact us:
Telephone 631-231-7269; Fax 631-231-8175
Web Site: http://www.novapublishers.com

NOTICE TO THE READER

The Publisher has taken reasonable care in the preparation of this book, but makes no expressed or implied warranty of any kind and assumes no responsibility for any errors or omissions. No liability is assumed for incidental or consequential damages in connection with or arising out of information contained in this book. The Publisher shall not be liable for any special, consequential, or exemplary damages resulting, in whole or in part, from the readers' use of, or reliance upon, this material.

Independent verification should be sought for any data, advice or recommendations contained in this book. In addition, no responsibility is assumed by the publisher for any injury and/or damage to persons or property arising from any methods, products, instructions, ideas or otherwise contained in this publication.

This publication is designed to provide accurate and authoritative information with regard to the subject matter covered herein. It is sold with the clear understanding that the Publisher is not engaged in rendering legal or any other professional services. If legal or any other expert assistance is required, the services of a competent person should be sought. FROM A DECLARATION OF PARTICIPANTS JOINTLY ADOPTED BY A COMMITTEE OF THE AMERICAN BAR ASSOCIATION AND A COMMITTEE OF PUBLISHERS.

LIBRARY OF CONGRESS CATALOGING-IN-PUBLICATION DATA

Available upon request

ISBN: 978-1-60692-188-3

Published by Nova Science Publishers, Inc. ✢ *New York*

CONTENTS

Preface		vii
Chapter 1	Guide to Purchasing Green Power	1
Chapter 2	The Greening of U.S. Corporations	77
Chapter 3	EPA's Green Power Partnership	139
Index		147

PREFACE

Today the energy sources used to create electricity differ in many ways, including in their environmental impacts. In the United States, conventional means of electricity generation use fossil or nuclear fuels—forms of power generation that impact human health and the environment through air emissions and other effects. Despite advances in pollution controls over the last 30 years, conventional power generation is still the nation's single largest source of industrial air pollution. Electricity markets are changing, however, offering cleaner ways of producing power and giving many consumers the ability to choose how their power is generated. One of these choices is power from renewable sources that is marketed as green power. Innovative organizations are encouraging the use of these new sources of green power and, at the same time, are reducing their own impact on the environment.In some parts of the United States, the deregulation of electricity has enabled consumers to choose the provider of their electric power and thus to buy green power from their chosen supplier. In regulated markets, too, hundreds of utilities now offer their customers the opportunity to purchase green power through green-pricing" programs. Even in areas where consumers cannot buy green power directly, renewable energy certificates (RECs) are available in every state to allow consumers to support green power. While no form of electric power generation is completely benign, electricity generated from renewable resources such as solar, wind, geothermal, small and low-impact hydro power, and biomass has proved to be environmentally preferable to electricity generated from conventional energy sources such as coal, oil, nuclear, and natural gas. The Guide to Purchasing Green Power focuses on electricity generated from renewable energy resources, both delivered through the grid and generated on-site. By buying green power instead of conventional power,consumers can reduce the environmental impact caused by their use of electricity and fossil fuel. For instance, on average, every kilowatt-hour (kWh) of renewable power avoids the emission of more than one pound of carbon dioxide. Because of the sheer quantities of energy involved,consumers of a large amount of electricity may have an enormous environmental impact. If the typical commercial facility switched to 100 percent renewable power or used RECs to offset emissions, this could amount to thousands of tons of emissions avoided each year. A wide range of organizations have purchased green power: federal, state, and local governments; universities;businesses; nonprofits; and individual consumers. By purchasing green power, these organizations are both helping the environment and meeting their own environmental goals. The many other benefits to buying green power range from financial benefits to public relations and even national security. As of the end of 2003, nearly 1,650 megawatts(MW) of new renewable generating capacity had been added to meet the United States' demand for green power. This capacity is enough to meet the annual electricity needs of more than 500,000 houses.Leading organizations are finding that green power is an effective part of a strategic energy management plan to achieve environmental, financial, and other goals. Successful energy management plans are often a "portfolio analysis" that considers options such as energy efficiency, load management, power purchases, on-site generation, and nonelectric (thermal) energy needs. As with any investment portfolio, the best mix of these options depends on the particular situation. Because buying green power is still relatively uncommon in today's energy markets and because these markets offer a wide range of choices, this book provides leading-research for organizations that have decided to buy green power but want help in figuring out how to do it, as well as for organizations that are still considering the merits of buying green power.

Chapter 1 - The *Guide to Purchasing Green Power* is intended for organizations that are considering the merits of buying green power as well as those that have decided to buy it and want help doing so. The *Guide* was written for a broad audience, including businesses, government agencies, universities, and all organizations wanting to diversify their energy supply and to reduce the environmental impact of their electricity use.

The *Guide* provides an overview of green power markets and describes the necessary steps to buying green power. This section summarizes the *Guide* to help readers find the information they need.

Part 1 describes the concepts of renewable energy and green power and discusses their differences from traditional energy sources. This section also summarizes recent changes in electricity markets.

Part 2 defines three types of green power products: renewable electricity, renewable energy certificates, and on- site renewable generation. Renewable electricity is generated using renewable energy resources and delivered through the utility grid; renewable energy certificates (RECs) represent the environmental, social, and other positive attributes of power generated by renewable resources; and on-site renewable generation is electricity generated using renewable energy resources at the end-user's facility.

Part 3 summarizes the benefits and costs of purchasing green power. Benefits include a financial hedge against various risks, improving relations with organizational stakeholders, helping the environment, and bolstering economic development and security. Conversely, green power may be more expensive than traditional power and present new contracting challenges.

Part 4 describes in detail the three main green power products, including the alternative renewable electricity products, the details of RECs transactions, and the technologies that can be used to harness on-site renewable resources.

Part 5 outlines the general steps needed to prepare to buy green power: identifying the key decision makers, gathering energy data, and choosing the specific green power options available to the purchaser's facilities.

Part discusses the steps to procure renewable electricity or renewable energy certificates: developing screening criteria, collecting product information, and drawing up a procurement plan.

Part describes the steps to establish an on-site renewable energy system: screening the technologies best suited to the purchaser's site, obtaining technical and financial assistance, creating a project plan, anticipating possible barriers, and installing and operating the on-site generation system.

Part explores ways of taking advantage of promotional opportunities after buying green power. This section covers promotion both inside and outside the organization and options for quantifying the environmental benefits of the purchase.

Parts 9 and 10 of the *Guide* conclude with a list of resources offering more information about all aspects of green power. Because electricity from renewable resources is relatively new and may be generated in a variety of ways, many institutions are working to facilitate the development of green power markets. Several of these organizations' programs—the U.S. Department of Energy's Federal Energy Management Program (FEMP), the U.S. Environmental Protection Agency's Green Power Partnership, the Sustainable Enterprise Program of the World Resources Institute (WRI), and the Green-e Renewable Energy Certification Program administered by the Center for Resource Solutions—worked together to write this purchasing guide. More information about these programs is available from the Web sites listed in chapter 10, Resources for Additional Information.

Finally, the appendix to the *Guide* discusses considerations specific to federal agencies that buy green power, particularly the procurement regulations that cover the purchase of green power.

In: Green Movement in Business
Editor: Karin E. Sanchez

ISBN: 978-1-60692-188-3
© 2009 Nova Science Publishers, Inc.

Chapter 1

GUIDE TO PURCHASING GREEN POWER

ABSTRACT

The *Guide to Purchasing Green Power* is intended for organizations that are considering the merits of buying green power as well as those that have decided to buy it and want help doing so. The *Guide* was written for a broad audience, including businesses, government agencies, universities, and all organizations wanting to diversify their energy supply and to reduce the environmental impact of their electricity use.

The *Guide* provides an overview of green power markets and describes the necessary steps to buying green power. This section summarizes the *Guide* to help readers find the information they need.

Part 1 describes the concepts of renewable energy and green power and discusses their differences from traditional energy sources. This section also summarizes recent changes in electricity markets.

Part 2 defines three types of green power products: renewable electricity, renewable energy certificates, and on-site renewable generation. Renewable electricity is generated using renewable energy resources and delivered through the utility grid; renewable energy certificates (RECs) represent the environmental, social, and other positive attributes of power generated by renewable resources; and on-site renewable generation is electricity generated using renewable energy resources at the end-user's facility.

Part 3 summarizes the benefits and costs of purchasing green power. Benefits include a financial hedge against various risks, improving relations with organizational stakeholders, helping the environment, and bolstering economic development and security. Conversely, green power may be more expensive than traditional power and present new contracting challenges.

Part 4 describes in detail the three main green power products, including the alternative renewable electricity products, the details of RECs transactions, and the technologies that can be used to harness on-site renewable resources.

Part 5 outlines the general steps needed to prepare to buy green power: identifying the key decision makers, gathering energy data, and choosing the specific green power options available to the purchaser's facilities.

Part discusses the steps to procure renewable electricity or renewable energy certificates: developing screening criteria, collecting product information, and drawing up a procurement plan.

Part describes the steps to establish an on-site renewable energy system: screening the technologies best suited to the purchaser's site, obtaining technical and financial assistance, creating a project plan, anticipating possible barriers, and installing and operating the on-site generation system.

Part explores ways of taking advantage of promotional opportunities after buying green power. This section covers promotion both inside and outside the organization and options for quantifying the environmental benefits of the purchase.

Parts 9 and 10 of the *Guide* conclude with a list of resources offering more information about all aspects of green power. Because electricity from renewable resources is relatively new and may be generated in a variety of ways, many institutions are working to facilitate the development of green power markets. Several of these organizations' programs—the U.S. Department of Energy's Federal Energy Management Program (FEMP), the U.S. Environmental Protection Agency's Green Power Partnership, the Sustainable Enterprise Program of the World Resources Institute (WRI), and the Green-e Renewable Energy Certification Program administered by the Center for Resource Solutions—worked together to write this purchasing guide. More information about these programs is available from the Web sites listed in chapter 10, Resources for Additional Information.

Finally, the appendix to the *Guide* discusses considerations specific to federal agencies that buy green power, particularly the procurement regulations that cover the purchase of green power.

1. INTRODUCTION

Today the energy sources used to create electricity differ in many ways, including in their environmental impacts. In the United States, conventional means of electricity generation use fossil or nuclear fuels— forms of power generation that impact human health and the environment through air emissions and other effects. Despite advances in pollution controls over the last 30 years, conventional power generation is still the nation's single largest source of industrial air pollution.

Electricity markets are changing, however, offering cleaner ways of producing power and giving many consumers the ability to choose how their power is generated. One of these choices is power from renewable sources that is marketed as green power. Innovative organizations are encouraging the use of these new sources of green power and, at the same time, are reducing their own impact on the environment.

In some parts of the United States, the deregulation of electricity has enabled consumers to choose the provider of their electric power and thus to buy green power from their chosen supplier. In regulated markets, too, hundreds of utilities now offer their customers the opportunity to purchase green power through "green-pricing" programs. Even in areas where consumers cannot buy green power directly, renewable energy certificates (RECs) are available in every state to allow consumers to support green power.

While no form of electric power generation is completely benign, electricity generated from renewable resources such as solar, wind, geothermal, small and low-impact hydropower, and biomass has proved to be environmentally preferable to electricity generated from conventional energy sources such as coal, oil, nuclear, and natural gas. The *Guide to Purchasing Green Power* focuses on electricity generated from renewable energy resources, both delivered through the grid and generated on-site. Although renewable energy can also be used for heating needs or for transportation fuels, the *Guide* does not address those applications.

By buying green power instead of conventional power, consumers can reduce the environmental impact caused by their use of electricity and fossil fuel. For instance, on average, every kilowatt-hour (kWh) of renewable power avoids the emission of more than one pound of carbon dioxide. Because of the sheer quantities of energy involved, consumers of a large amount of electricity may have an enormous environmental impact. If the typical commercial facility switched to 100 percent renewable power or used RECs to offset emissions, this could amount to thousands of tons of emissions avoided each year.

A wide range of organizations have purchased green power: federal, state, and local governments; universities; businesses; nonprofits; and individual consumers. By purchasing green power, these organizations are both helping the environment and meeting their own environmental goals. The many other benefits to buying green power range from financial benefits to public relations and even national security. As of the end of 2003, nearly 1,650 megawatts (MW) of new renewable generating capacity had been added to meet the United States' demand for green power. This capacity is enough to meet the annual electricity needs of more than 500,000 houses.

Leading organizations are finding that green power is an effective part of a strategic energy management plan to achieve environmental, financial, and other goals. Successful energy management plans are often a "portfolio analysis" that considers options such as energy efficiency, load management, power purchases, on-site generation, and nonelectric (thermal) energy needs. As with any investment portfolio, the best mix of these options depends on the particular situation.

Because buying green power is still relatively uncommon in today's energy markets and because these markets offer a wide range of choices, the *Guide* is intended for organizations that have decided to buy green power but want help in figuring out how to do it, as well as for organizations that are still considering the merits of buying green power.

The *Guide to Purchasing Green Power* addresses the following commonly asked questions:

- What are renewable energy and green power? (p. 4)
- What benefits will my green power purchase bring? (p. 5)
- How do I make a business case for buying green power? (p. 5)
- What is the cost of green power? (p. 6)
- What are the options for purchasing green power? (p. 9)
- What is the importance of product certification and verification? (p. 9)
- What are the best ways of buying green power? (p. 16)
- How should an organization choose a green power product? (p. 13)
- What are the steps to installing on-site renewable generation? (p. 21)
- What is the best way of telling the organization, employees, and community about the benefits of green power? (p. 25)

2. THE DEFINITION OF GREEN POWER

Renewable energy is derived from natural sources that replenish themselves over short periods of time. These resources include the sun, wind, moving water, organic plant and waste material (biomass), and the earth's heat (geothermal). This renewable energy can be used to generate electricity as well as for other applications. For example, biomass may be used as boiler fuel to generate steam heat; solar energy may be used to heat water or for passive space heating; and landfill methane gas can be used for heating or cooking.

Although the environmental impacts of renewable energy are generally minimal, these power sources still do have some effect on the environment. For example, biomass resources are converted to electricity through combustion, which emits some air pollutants. Hydroelectric dams can flood the surrounding land and impede the passage of fish. Compared with conventional power, however, renewable power generally avoids, or at least significantly reduces, the adverse environmental impacts of conventional electricity generation.

The term *green power* is used in a number of different ways. In the broadest sense, green power refers to environmentally preferable energy and energy technologies, both electric and thermal. This definition of green power includes many things, from solar photovoltaic systems to wind turbines to fuel cells for automobiles.

Although renewable resources do more than generate electricity, green power is most commonly used in a narrower, marketing, sense to refer specifically to *electricity* from renewable resources. In the context of the *Guide to Purchasing Green Power*, the term *green power* refers to electricity products that include significant proportions of electricity generated from energy resources that are both renewable and environmentally preferable.

In the *Guide*, green power includes the following three products:

- "Renewable electricity" is generated using renewable energy resources and is delivered through the utility grid.
- "Renewable Energy Certificates" (RECs) represent the environmental, social, and other positive attributes of power generated by renewable resources.
- "On-site renewable generation" refers to electricity generated using renewable energy resources at the end-user's facility.

Note that the terms *green power, environmentally preferable,* and *renewable energy* may be used in slightly different ways, which differ primarily according to the varying assessments of the environmental impacts of harnessing specific resources and of the relative significance of each impact. The exact definitions of these terms, while always important, take on added significance when dealing with state and federal government requirements or determining eligibility for government and utility incentives. For more discussion of how each of the organizations that collaborated on this document defines green power, please refer to their Web sites, listed in Chapter 10.

> Helping Define Green Power
>
> To help consumers more easily identify green power products, the "Green-e" Renewable Energy Certification Program is working to build market-based, consensus definitions for environmentally-preferable renewable electricity and renewable energy certificates. The Green-e program, administered by the non-profit Center for Resource Solutions (CRS), certifies and verifies renewable electricity products in competitive power markets, as well as utility green pricing programs and in national markets for RECs. Further details about Green-e certification are available from the Green-e Web sites listed in Chapter 10.

3. THE BENEFITS AND COSTS OF GREEN POWER

The Benefits

Green power can help many organizations meet environmental, financial, stakeholder relations, economic development, and national security objectives.

Environmental
- Avoid environmental impacts.

Green power and renewable energy avoid most of the environmental impacts associated with traditional power generation, helping protect human health and the health of the environment.

Financial
Provide a hedge against risks posed by

- Electricity price instability. Purchasing electricity generated by renewable energy resources creates a financial hedge against unstable or rising fossil fuel prices by diversifying a consumer's energy portfolio. Wind, geothermal, hydro, and solar energy are not subject to the rise and fall of fuel costs. For these reasons, renewable electricity can offer a fixed price over the long term.
- Fuel supply disruptions. On-site renewable generation can reduce the risk of disruptions in fuel supplies resulting from transportation difficulties or international conflict.
- Additional environmental regulation. To address global climate change and regional air quality issues, federal and state regulations have been proposed that would effectively increase the price of conventional electricity. But green power would be largely unaffected by these regulations, resulting in more stable prices over the long run.
- Electricity blackouts. Organizations that need highly reliable power usually use on-site power generation, such as diesel engines and gas turbines, for their facilities in the event of a power outage. On-site renewable generation can provide this backup power without fossil fuel emissions. Some renewable sources, however, require battery storage or other backup devices for essential electrical services during an outage.

Stakeholder Relations
- Meet organizational environmental objectives. Reducing an organization's environmental impact is one of the main motivations for buying green power. For example, buying green power can help meet greenhouse gas reduction targets. If an organization is interested in ISO-14001 certification for environmental performance, a program for reducing energy-related emissions will be an important part of this certification process.
- Demonstrate civic leadership. Being among the first in a community to purchase green power is a demonstration of civic leadership. It makes a statement that an organization is willing to

act on its stated environmental or social goals. These purchases also demonstrate an organization's responsiveness to its customers, the majority of whom favor renewable energy (see chapter 10 for more details).
- Generate positive publicity. Buying green power affords an opportunity for public recognition and public relations that advertising and media relations cannot buy. Companies that are in the public eye need to be responsive to the concerns of environmentally conscious customers, shareholders, regulators, and other constituents. Groups promoting green power, such as the EPA's Green Power Partnership, provide assistance in reaching broad audiences to convey the benefits of green power purchases.
- Improve employee morale. Progressive action and leadership on environmental issues like renewable energy may improve employee morale, which in turn can reduce employee turnover, attract new employees, and improve productivity. In a survey of 464 organizations, sponsored by the National Wind Coordinating Committee, improving employee morale was cited as the third most important motivation for buying green power.
- Differentiate products or services. By purchasing green power, a company may be able to differentiate its products or services by, for example, offering them as "made with certified renewable energy" or "climate neutral." Purchasers of green power can also join their power supplier to market their products together. In addition, purchasers of products certified by the Center for Resource Solutions Green-e program can display the Green-e logo on their product packaging to indicate the share of renewable energy used by the company or in its production.

Economic Development and National Security
- *Stimulate local economies.* Because renewable resources are typically local, jobs are created to install and operate renewable generation facilities. Renewable power facilities also increase the local tax base and can provide income for farmers and rural communities. The renewable energy industry may be an important growth opportunity in mature, postindustrial economies like that of the United States.

- *Increase fuel diversity.* Renewable energy diversifies the nation's fuel resources—a good way to manage risk—and, because renewable resources are indigenous, reduces its dependence on imported fuels.
- *Reduce infrastructure vulnerability.* The wide distribution of most renewable energy resources improves the robustness of energy systems by reducing the country's reliance on a vulnerable, centralized energy infrastructure.
- *Market transformation.* By purchasing green power now, organizations can reduce long-term production costs and transform markets for renewable energy technologies. Most renewable technologies are not yet produced in great volumes, but their production costs should drop significantly as their production volume increases, which in turn will attract more purchases.

Price Stability of Green Power

IBM has a longstanding corporate energy management program that is intended to improve the environment and reduce energy costs. The energy managers at IBM's Austin, Texas facility furthered both these goals by signing up for Austin Energy's GreenChoice® program in 2001. Under GreenChoice, the normal fossil fuel charge on the customer's bill is replaced by a green power charge for the amount of green power that the customer chooses to buy. Unlike the fossil fuel charge, which fluctuates over time, the green power charge is fixed until 2011. As it turned out, Austin Energy's fuel charge for conventional power spiked in 2001 and IBM saved $20,000 in its first year in the program. With the fuel charge having increased again in 2004, IBM expects to save over $60,000 per year. Moreover, the cost stability provided by this contract made it easier to manage the facility's energy budget.

> ### Demonstrating Leadership
>
> On January 1, 2003, Dyess Air Force Base (AFB), Texas, became the largest consumer of renewable electricity at a single site in the nation. The base now purchases 100 percent wind-generated electricity for all its electrical needs, resulting in approximately 80 million kWh of wind energy generated annually. The Dyess energy managers decided to make such a large purchase in order to demonstrate leadership to other agencies in meeting the federal renewable purchase goal. This builds on earlier, award-winning improvements that the base made in energy efficiency and water conservation.

The Costs

Green power may cost more than standard power sources, for several reasons.

Price Premiums

Renewable energy has usually been more expensive than conventional power sources. These higher costs are largely due to the relative immaturity of renewable technologies and their concentration in niche markets, compared with conventional energy sources. Chapter 6 of the *Guide* suggests ways of minimizing these costs in conjunction with a procurement plan. Nonetheless, despite the currently higher prices, the cost of renewable energy is falling as the growing demand justifies the expansion of manufacturing facilities and reduces production costs. Figure 1 illustrates the dramatic decline in the cost of wind power over the last two decades, while figure 2 shows that several renewable power technologies are now nearly cost competitive with conventional sources.

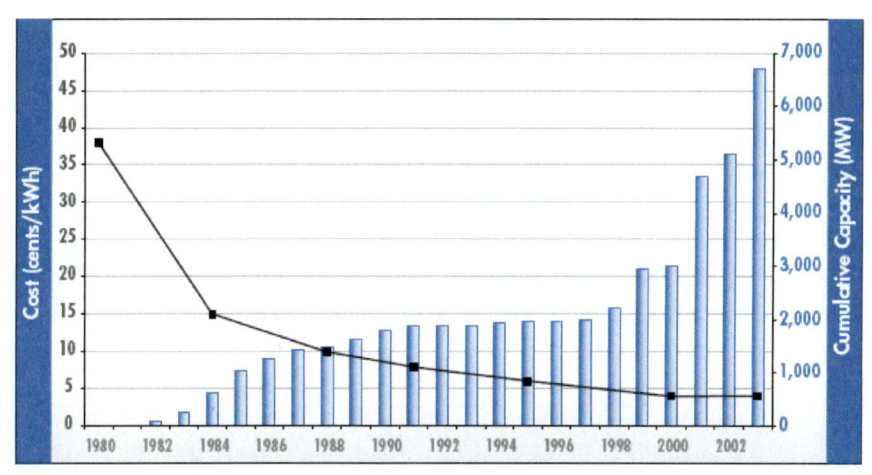

Source: American Wind Energy Association, 2003.
Cost figures are averages and will vary by project.

Figure 1. Wind Energy Costs Fall as Installed Capacity Increases.

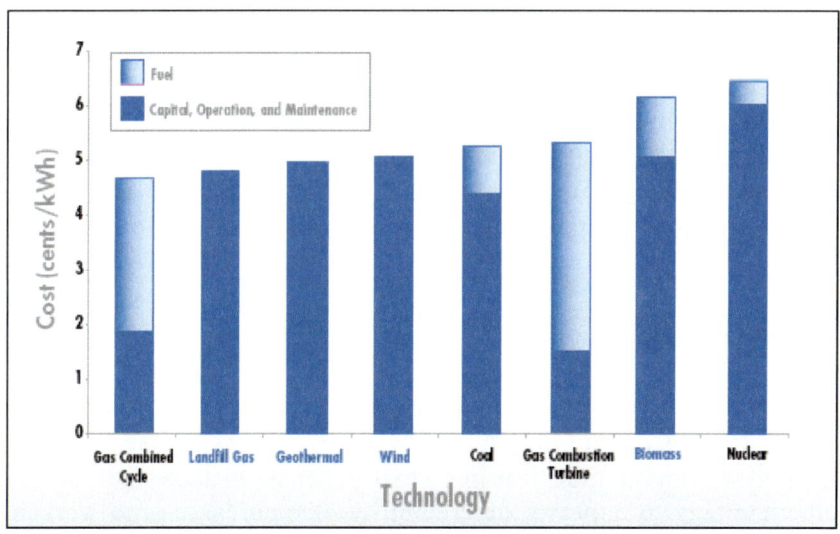

Source: Energy Information Administration Annual Energy Outlook, 2004.
Solar technologies are not included because their costs are application specific.

Figure 2. Cost Comparison of New Power Plants Using Renewable and Conventional Electricity Technologies.

The actual price for green power depends on a number of factors, including the availability and quality of the resource, the market price of conventional electricity, the availability of subsidies to encourage green power, and the quantity and terms of the contract. Generally, the price of green power ranges from less than that of the standard power mix, especially in competitive markets and where state subsidies exist, up to one to four cents more per kilowatt-hour.

When the market price of conventional electricity is high, purchasers of green power at a fixed price may actually save money. Of course, when the market price of conventional electricity drops, they will be paying a premium.

Contracting Challenges

Green power may also be more difficult than conventional power for an organization to purchase, causing transaction costs in addition to any price premiums. Although organizations that are buying green power for the first time may need to invest extra effort, these costs fall significantly over time as the electricity purchasers gain experience. Following the information and strategies provided in this guidebook, particularly chapter 6, should help reduce the contracting challenges faced by new purchasers of green power. In addition, sample contract templates are publicly available to help buyers avoid difficulties in signing a green power contract (see chapter 10, Resources for Additional Information).

Public Relations Risk

Some stakeholders may regard the purchase of green power as a token effort or "green washing." Organizations can avoid this criticism by buying green power as part of a broader environmental management program. Another strategy to improve the credibility of a purchase is to work with third- party organizations for independent auditing, endorsement, and minimum purchasing benchmarks.

4. OPTIONS FOR PURCHASING GREEN POWER

Green power can be purchased in several different ways. The main distinction among the options depends on where the power generation equipment is located: on the power grid or on-site at the facility. For electricity delivered over the power grid, the status of utility restructuring in that state will determine whether an organization can buy green power from either the existing utility or a competitive power supplier. Even if the state has no green power marketers or the utility does not offer a green power option, an organization can buy renewable energy certificates (RECs). For on-site renewable generation, the renewable energy resources available at that site (e.g., solar, wind, biomass) are the main factors determining the project's feasibility.

These options are not mutually exclusive. Some organizations may want to first buy a green power product requiring less financial commitment (such as an electricity product with a smaller fraction of renewable content). Over time, this can be supplemented by larger purchases or the installation of on- site generation. As discussed later, RECs can be a good place to start because of the ease and flexibility of the purchase.

Renewable Electricity Products

Renewable electricity products—offered by either the utility or the power marketer that provides the organization's power—can be structured in several different ways. The availability of each of these products varies according to the facility's location and the electricity provider's offerings. Although each product differs slightly, most renewable electricity products fall into one of two types.

- *Fixed energy quantity block.* A block is a quantity of 100 percent renewable electricity, often 100 kilowatt- hours (kWh), offered for a fixed monthly price. The price is often expressed as a price premium above the price of conventional power. Customers usually may sign up for as many blocks as they wish, with the monthly cost of these products based on how many blocks they buy. This type of product is available in some competitive markets but is more often found in regulated utility green-pricing programs.

- *Percentage of monthly use.* Customers may choose renewable electricity to supply a fixed percentage of their monthly electricity use. In practice, this usually results in the purchase of a blend of renewable and conventional power. This is typically priced as a premium on a cents per kWh basis over the standard rate or as a fixed charge per kWh. The monthly cost for these products varies with energy use and the percentage of renewable energy chosen.

Some renewable electricity products require a fixed monthly fee to support a given amount of renewable generation capacity, or even require contributing to a renewable energy fund that finances renewable projects. These products can be an effective way to assist the green power industry but do not, however, result in a metered amount of renewable electricity being generated, which is necessary to quantify the environmental benefits of the green power purchase. For this reason, these products are not discussed further in this guide. Chapter 6 provides more details about implementing a renewable electricity purchase.

The Role of Product Certification

One of the major concerns with buying green power is ensuring that purchasers get what they pay for. It can be difficult to substantiate claims made about the quantity and characteristics of the product purchased. Also, it is important to ensure that two organizations are not claiming to have purchased the same green power, or are double-counting the same green power benefits. Moreover, purchasers may be unable to ensure public acceptance of their purchase and avoid criticism from external stakeholders without independent information about the product. Third-party certification addresses these concerns by setting standards for green power products in the following areas:

Minimum levels of environmentally-acceptable renewable resources,
Overall environmental impact,
Ethical conduct for suppliers, including advertising claims and regular reporting.

Third-party certification usually also requires independent verification by an auditor to document that green power purchased equals green power supplied, and to verify other resource claims. Visit www.green-e.org for additional information about third-party certification and verification.

Renewable Energy Certificates (RECs)

A REC represents the environmental, social, and other positive attributes of power generated by renewable resources. These attributes may be sold separately from the underlying commodity electricity (figure 3). For example, RECs represent the reduced emissions of renewable generation compared with those of conventional generation. The actual power that is sold is no longer considered "green" and is treated like any other commodity electricity. In practice, REC transactions can take many forms in addition to that shown in figure 3. For more details about REC transactions, see chapter 10, Resources for Additional Information.

Because RECs are sold separately from electricity, they can be purchased from locations anywhere, enabling organizations to choose renewable power even if their local utility or power marketer does not offer a green power product. Although theoretically there are no geographic constraints on buying RECs, accounting systems to record and track the exchange of certificates are not yet available everywhere. In addition, the location of environmental benefits may be important to some purchasers. A variety of REC products are available from local and national sources.

Customers do not need to switch from their current electricity supplier to purchase certificates, and they can buy RECs based on a fixed amount of energy (or carbon footprint) rather than on their daily or monthly load profile. Because certificates are independent of the customer's energy use, load profile, and the delivery of energy to the customer's facility, they provide greater flexibility than purchasing energy and attributes bundled together as renewable power. One drawback to RECs is that they do not offer the same financial hedge value that some other green power products provide.

Purchasing RECs for special events

RECs can offer flexibility by allowing a buyer to offset electricity used for special events, such as conferences, rather than requiring long-term purchases. The Department of Energy used this approach for the Labs for the 21st Century annual meeting, where the conference organizers purchased green power certificates equivalent to 100% of the energy consumed at the meeting. Because special events inherently generate a lot of publicity, the public and employee relations benefit from this approach can be significant.

Price premiums for certificates may be lower than those for renewable electricity products, for several reasons: (1) RECs have no geographic constraints and therefore can provide access to the least expensive renewable resources; (2) the supplier does not have to deliver the power to the REC purchaser with the associated transmission and distribution costs; and (3) the supplier is not responsible for meeting the purchaser's electricity needs on a real-time basis.

An alternative way to buy RECs is through a subscription, or "future RECs," which involves an up-front purchase of RECs to be generated in the future by a new renewable facility. The advantage of this approach is that it promotes new renewable facilities by providing up-front financial assistance for their development and construction. In return, the purchaser receives the RECs as they are generated over an extended period of years. Compared to annually buying RECS close to the time they are generated, the subscription method emphasizes the up-front payment for a future stream of RECs. The additional risk of this approach is that the plant might not be constructed, and buyers should investigate what remedy the seller proposes in such an event. As with all products, independent product certification and verification of the claims made is an important aspect to consider.

For a company or institution with operations and offices in multiple locations, purchasing RECs can consolidate the procurement of renewable energy, thus eliminating the need to buy renewable electricity for different facilities through multiple suppliers. Chapter 6 provides more details about purchasing RECs.

On-Site Renewable Generation

In addition to buying renewable electricity from a utility or buying renewable energy certificates, organizations can install renewable power generation at their facilities.

They can either buy the system outright or install a system that is owned by another party and buy the electricity as it is generated.

On-site renewable generation offers advantages such as enhanced reliability, power quality, and protection against price volatility, as well as a visible demonstration of environmental commitment. In many states, electricity generated with on-site renewable generation may be sold back to the grid at the same price at which power is bought, through a process called *net metering*. This arrangement may improve the financial return for on-site renewable power systems, although net metering is often limited to small installations.

On-site renewable energy technologies for power generation include photovoltaic panels, wind turbines, fuel cells, and biomass combustion. Large facilities sited near a municipal landfill or sewage treatment plant may be able to use recovered methane gas for on-site electricity and/or heat production. The following describes each of these options in more detail:

- *Solar.* Photovoltaic (PV) cells and modules can be configured to almost any size from a few kilowatts up to more than one megawatt. On-site photovoltaic cells may be situated on schools, homes, community facilities, and commercial buildings. Photovoltaic cells can be made part of a building, displacing other building material costs, for example, roofing shingles or car park shading.
- *Wind.* Wind turbines vary in size. A typical small unit provides fewer than 25 kW, whereas large turbines range from 500 kW to more than 3 MW. On-site applications are usually only possible in nonurban areas, and often require zoning permits to exceed 35-foot height restrictions (a tower for a 250 kW turbine is 130 feet high with a blade sweep of 98 feet). Such installations usually require approximately one acre of land per turbine and wind speeds that average 15 mph at a 50-meter height. In addition, placing turbines near tall buildings is inadvisable because the building may create wind turbulence that can disrupt the turbines' performance.
- *Landfill and sewage methane gas.* Methane gas derived from landfills or sewage treatment plants may be used to generate electricity. Methane gas also may be generated using digesters that operate on manure or agricultural wastes. The methane gas is then converted to electricity using an internal combustion engine, gas turbine (depending on the quality and quantity of the gas), direct combustion boiler and steam turbine generator set, microturbine unit, or other power conversion technology. Most methane gas projects produce from 0.5 to 4 MW of electrical output.
- *Biomass.* Biomass is plant material burned in a boiler to drive a steam turbine to produce electricity. This system is good for

producing combined heat and power (CHP) at facilities with large thermal loads. Biomass projects are best suited to locations with abundant biomass resources (often using waste products from the forest industry or agriculture).
- *Fuel cells.* Fuel cells are another way of producing power. They emit essentially no air pollution and are more efficient than other forms of generation. But they cannot be considered a renewable resource unless they operate on a renewably generated fuel, such as digester gas or hydrogen derived from PV or wind power.

On-site generation case study

Car-maker BMW pipes methane gas 9.5 miles from a landfill to serve the electric and thermal needs of its manufacturing facility in Greer, South Carolina. Rather than invest in new internal combustion engines to generate electricity, BMW converted four turbines that previously ran on purchased natural gas. By recovering the waste heat from the turbines, the 5 MW combined heat and power project satisfies 80% of the facility's thermal needs, as well as 25% of its electricity use.

In this era of power reliability problems and national security concerns, on-site renewable generation offers important advantages over central-station and fossil-fueled power plants. Moreover, on-site generation can be designed to provide backup power for critical loads when power from the grid is interrupted, as well as when the renewable resource is not available. This ability to operate independently of the power grid is a great advantage, particularly at remote facilities. Because renewable generation technologies tend to be modular and used on a small scale, the on-site generation system can be designed to enhance the redundancy and diversity of a facility's energy supply.

On-site renewable generation has higher capital costs and lower operating costs compared with installing fossil-fueled generation. Although these costs may make the initial investment in on-site generation more difficult to justify, once that investment has been made, the annual budgets for maintaining the system are much easier to justify (compared with purchasing renewable electricity), which makes it easier to sustain a commitment to renewable power.

An organization that installs its own generation capability may have problems with the requirements for connecting to the utility distribution system, commonly referred to as *interconnection*. Standardizing the interconnection rules may help in the future, but in some cases, the rules for large generators are unnecessarily burdensome for small installations. In recognition of this problem—and to encourage on-site generation—a few states have simplified their interconnection rules; in addition, national standards are being drawn up that may ease interconnection. Net-metering laws, which allow an owner of an on-site power system to sell electricity back to the grid, usually provide more lenient interconnection rules for small installations. Chapter 7 provides more details about procuring an on-site renewable generation system.

5. STEPS TO PURCHASING GREEN POWER

To buy green power, an organization first should determine whether green power will help fulfill its energy needs, identify the best products for its particular situation, and decide how to procure those products. Figure 4 describes the steps in this process.

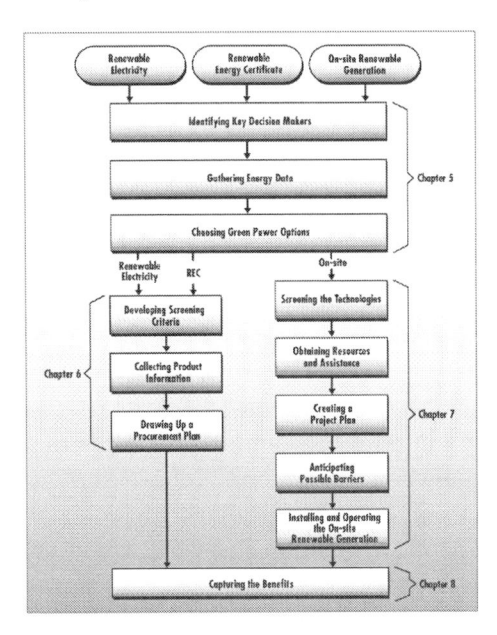

Figure 4. Steps to a Successful Green Power Project.

The preliminary steps, described in this section, are the same for all types of green power products. The final steps differ for purchased green power products and on-site renewable generation. These steps are explained in later chapters of this guide.

Identifying Key Decision Makers

The people in an organization who are interested in green power may be high-level decision makers as well as staff from the purchasing, facilities/energy management, environmental health and safety, legal, corporate relations, and/or marketing departments. Their interests and concerns need to be addressed. Experience has demonstrated that not doing so often leads to disagreements later in the process, whereas including these interested people in the early planning stages goes a long way toward addressing their concerns. These departments (such as environmental or marketing) may also contribute funds to help pay for green power.

It is important to designate a contact person who can draw on expertise from throughout the organization. Which departments are chosen to participate will probably depend on the type of products being considered. It also is important to involve senior management in the planning and decision process. In some cases, the greatest advocate of buying green power is an executive such as a CEO or president. With this high-level support, buying and promoting green power is much easier. Some organizations involve their employees (or students, in the case of educational institutions) in selecting the green power products.

At this early stage it is necessary to decide on the objectives for purchasing green power.

- Why is the organization considering green power?
- What does it hope to get from it?
- What selection criteria are important to the organization?
- Is buying new generation more important than maintaining the generation that has been in place for many years?
- Is independent certification and verification important to the organization?

Gathering Energy Data

The organization should take an inventory of its energy use, including both electricity and fossil fuels. Its monthly energy use can be calculated from the utility bills for each facility or business unit and for the entire organization. These data will help (1) find where energy can be saved, (2) determine how much green power to buy, and (3) evaluate the environmental impacts of the organization's electricity use. Monthly electricity consumption data are the most important, while peak demand and interval-meter data are useful if available. The organization should study its consumption data over the past year before specifying its requirements. Outside consultants or organizations can help with these steps.

As mentioned earlier, green power can be considered part of an energy portfolio that includes energy efficiency upgrades, load management, combined heat and power, and green power. The more an organization's energy requirements can be reduced, the less green power it will need to buy to achieve a given objective, which in turn makes green power more affordable. Some organizations that have bought green power have saved enough from energy efficiency upgrades to enable them to pay the higher price of green power.

Many resources are available to help improve the energy efficiency of buildings and equipment. A good starting point is the ENERGY STAR Portfolio Manager, an online tool that compares a building's energy usage with that of similar buildings. The ENERGY STAR Web site (www.energystar.gov) also offers simple energy-saving tips and a directory of energy services companies to provide additional assistance, such as a facility energy audit.

An organization's annual energy consumption can be used to calculate the emissions associated with its current use and estimate the emissions that could be displaced by buying green power. The EPA's Green Power Partnership offers an online tool to help estimate emissions from an organization's electricity use (www.epa.gov/cleanenergy/power rofiler.htm).

Choosing Green Power Options

The next step is finding the appropriate green power solutions for the organization. Another goal of this step is becoming familiar with the electricity markets in the organization's area and the available green power technologies.

Paying for green power

Catholic University of America (CUA) has been pursuing energy conservation aggressively for the past eight years, utilizing performance contracting with guaranteed savings. Without an increase in its energy budget, CUA has still come in under budget for six years. CUA decided to use some of the savings to purchase 4 million kWh of wind power (the output of one turbine) for a five-year period. This purchase supplies nearly 12% of the university's total electricity, and the cost is the equivalent of buying each student one soda per month.

The first decision is whether to generate power on-site and/or to purchase power or RECs from outside vendors. The main differences between these options are the ease and cost of implementation, the need for capital investment, the ability to hedge risk, and the length of time over which one realizes the benefits. On-site renewable generation requires an upfront investment (as part of either a financed project or a capital appropriation), but the reduction in the consumption of conventional energy can last for as many as 30 years. Renewable electricity purchases and renewable energy certificates, however, require no up-front capital and are relatively easy to procure, but they deliver benefits only for the term of the purchase contract.

An organization's motivations for purchasing green power will help decide which costs and benefits are most important and thus which type of green power is most appropriate. For example, an organization wanting to manage fuel price risk may be more interested in buying fixed-price renewable electricity. An organization to which the reliability of its power supply is most important may be more interested in on-site renewable generation. These options can also be combined. For instance, an organization might install on-site generation to meet part of its electrical needs and purchase RECs to offset some or all of its remaining electricity usage. Likewise, organizations with facilities in multiple locations must select the appropriate green power product for each site.

The choice of green power options is determined partly by the electricity market structure in the state in which the facility is located. For renewable electricity, if the state's electricity market has been restructured, an organization can probably choose both its supplier and the product it prefers. Each state has different rules governing power marketers, and the level of competition varies among the states. If the organization's state electricity market has not been restructured, the local utility may offer a renewable electricity option (sometimes called utility green pricing). Large electricity purchasers may be able to work with their local utility or electricity provider to tailor a product to meet their needs.

> Assembling a list of green power products offered in a specific area
>
> - Perhaps the most complete source of information is the U.S. Department of Energy's Green Power Network Web site (www.eere.energy.gov/greenpower).
> - Many state governments, often the public utilities commission, maintain a list of power marketers offering green power products in their state.
> - Organizations with facilities in several states should use a national locator such as EPA's Green Power Locator (www.epa.gov/greenpower/locator.htm) or the Green-e "Pick your Power" locator (www.greene.org/your_e_choices/pyp.html). The latter is also useful for locating certified products.
> - Smaller facilities (such as retail stores) may find it easier to have a single point of contact compiling this information and making it available across the entire organization. Larger facilities (such as factories or research campuses) often have enough expertise to gather information and negotiate contracts on their own.
> - See Section 10 for more resources.

For on-site renewable generation, the organization should assess the renewable energy resources available at its facility, including the quality of wind and solar resources, the availability of biomass fuel or landfill gas, and siting constraints (such as space limitations or shading from neighboring buildings). The cost of conventional power at the facility also is important to consider. The organization should read over its utility's and state's interconnection rules to make sure there are no obvious provisions that would prohibit grid-connected, on-site generation. The goal at this stage is to eliminate any renewable options that are clearly not feasible for the organization.

6. PROCURING RENEWABLE ELECTRICITY AND RENEWABLE ENERGY CERTIFICATES

Developing Criteria for Screening Suppliers and Products

To help select both the green power supplier and the product, it is helpful to develop specific criteria for judging the alternatives. These criteria may be ranked, keeping in mind the goals identified early in the process when the project team was assembled.

For selecting green power suppliers, the following criteria may be helpful:

- *Reputation.* A supplier's reputation is influenced by factors such as how well it honors its commitments, how easy it is to work with, and how well it is viewed by the industry. Assessing a supplier's reputation may require references and a perusal of the energy industry's literature. Environmental groups also may have information about the supplier.
- *Financial strength.* To research the financial health of a power supplier, look at its Web site and perhaps its annual report, SEC filings, and bond ratings.
- *Location.* If buying green power from a local supplier is important, call the supplier and find out where its headquarters and branch offices are located. Public utility commissions' Web sites often have contact information for registered retail suppliers.
- *Product choice.* Some suppliers offer several green power products, varying in the amount of renewable power, types of resources, and the like. If a supplier offers a choice of green power products, this may enable the organization to

change the product it purchases in the future without having to search for a new supplier and negotiate a new contract.
- *Social responsibility.* Determining a supplier's social values and commitment to environmental conservation requires some research. The supplier's Web site is a good place to start. Organizations should review the supplier's annual report or environmental report, examine its other electricity products, and review its other business activities.

For green power products, consider the following criteria:

- *Price.* Green power prices may be quoted in total cents per kilowatt-hour or in extra cents per kilowatt-hour (incremental to the standard power rate). If the organization is in a regulated utility's service territory, compare the price of green power with the price of conventional power. In competitive markets, compare the price of green power with that of electric service under standard utility rates, that of electric service under the lowest-price competitive alternative, and that of the electric service that the organization is currently receiving. Also make sure to determine whether the price is fixed over time or fluctuates with changes in standard power rates (some utility green-pricing program participants are exempt from variable fuel charges).
- *Percentage of renewable energy.* For a particular green power product, the resource mix can range from 1 to 100 percent renewable power. When buying certificates or block products, an organization can still calculate the percentage of its energy use served by renewable power.
- *Percentage of new or incremental renewable sources.* Although it is important to support existing renewable generation, many experts argue that only new generation provides incremental environmental benefits. "New" renewable resources refer to renewable facilities that have been created specifically for the green power market. Existing facilities presumably sold power into the grid before a particular green power purchase and would continue to do so. Therefore, purchasing power from the existing facilities may not change the composition or the environmental impact of the region's generation mix. Besides the direct impact of purchases from new renewable sources, these purchases also create

the demand necessary for constructing additional renewable resources.

In some situations, however, buying power from existing renewable generation facilities can provide support for existing facilities that otherwise would have been underutilized or possibly even shut down, thus preventing their displacement by dirtier nonrenewable plants. When the demand for green power exceeds the supply, purchasing from existing facilities can eventually lead to the installation of new renewable generation capacity.

In states that have adopted a renewable portfolio standard (RPS), electricity providers are required to include a minimal percentage of renewable electricity in their standard product offering. Renewable electricity products create additional environmental benefits only if the power purchased is not already part of the provider's minimal RPS requirement.

- Renewable energy/resource mix. A renewable energy/resource mix refers to the kinds of resources used in the green power product. For example, is the product generated from wind, biomass, solar, geothermal, or hydro? Some resources have a greater environmental impact than others do, with different associated costs. Wind, solar, and geothermal power usually are the most environmentally preferable energy sources. Each is renewable and nonpolluting, with little impact on the land or local habitats. Certain environmental groups regard some types of hydropower, biomass, and municipal solid waste as less desirable. Hydropower dams may drastically alter river habitats and fish populations; biomass facilities may emit significant quantities of NOx; and burning municipal solid waste may release heavy metals and other toxins into the environment.

It also is important to check the environmental characteristics of any nonrenewable generation resources, as they will contribute to the overall environmental impact of the power purchased. One advantage of buying Green-e certified power is that the certification requires a product's nonrenewable resources to be, on average, cleaner than those of the local system power.

- Length of contract. Some buyers prefer a short-term contract in case the market changes and better offers come along. But an

organization may be able to lock in a lower price if it signs a multiyear contract. A longer-term contract may also offer greater price stability. When determining the value of price stability, be aware of "typical" market fluctuations in power prices and how the price of renewable electricity can vary. Finally, a contract may include options for renewal, which can offer flexibility in the future.
- Third-party certification and verification. A green power product can be certified and verified by an independent third party. Such certification can provide credibility and confirmation of the product's environmental value. Visit www.green-e.org for more information about certification.
- Location of generation. In order to support the local economy and to contribute local environmental benefits, some organizations may prefer local or in-state renewable generation. Some renewable electricity products, however, use resources located out-of-state, and renewable energy certificates may be based on generation located nationally or even internationally.
- Specific generation facility. Some green power providers generate their power at a specific site, such as a nearby wind farm. These products, such as the annual output of one particular wind turbine, offer the benefit of being more tangible because they are associated with an identifiable generating facility.

Collecting Product Information

A good place to start collecting information about specific green power options is the many Internet sources listed in this *Guide*. Be sure to collect enough information to answer the decision criteria listed earlier. For useful comparisons, the information should be as consistent as possible among suppliers and among products. A good way to find consistent information is through an exploratory letter or a request for information (RFI) addressed to specific suppliers.

In many states, competing electricity suppliers are required to provide an electricity label—like a list of food ingredients— that provides information in a standard format and makes product comparisons easier. This information is generally available from the state's public utility commission. Another source of public information is third-party certifiers, such as Green-e, Environmental Resources Trust, or Climate Neutral Network, which provide information about the products they have certified to meet minimum environmental standards. All Green-e certified products give standardized product content labels to prospective customers.

The next step is estimating the cost of green power for the organization and calculating the cost/benefit ratio. For help finding data, contact one of the organizations that sponsored this guidebook (listed in chapter 10).

Creating a Procurement Plan

A procurement plan documents the project team's decisions and addresses possible problems in buying green power. A procurement plan can also help convince others in the organization that purchasing green power is a wise choice.

The main audience for the procurement plan is the managers who need to support the purchase decision. Their support should be secured as early in the process as possible. As soon as the team can show the costs and benefits of purchasing green power to the organization, they should present their information to management. Expect the managers to ask about the products the organization would buy, their cost, and their benefits. Also find out whether management might limit a green power purchase or whether they would buy more aggressively.

Besides providing the information that management needs to make the decision, a procurement plan can also help overcome resistance to green power within the organization. Some organizations have outdated perceptions of the reliability of renewable energy technologies, misunderstandings about using an intermittent resource, or worries about the cost. As part of the procurement process, the project team will probably need to educate others about these topics and the benefits of green power. The organizations that sponsored this guidebook can provide helpful information to overcome these misconceptions.

The scope and detail of the procurement plan will depend on the organization's needs and requirements, but it should address the following:

Scope of Procurement

Specify the amount of power that will be purchased (as either a fixed amount of money for renewable purchases or a percentage of total power use) and for which facilities. If this procurement is a trial that may lead to additional purchases in the future, spell out the criteria that will be used to judge the trial's success. Also discuss whatever is known at this point about future procurement phases.

Expected Benefits

Keeping in mind the general benefits outlined earlier in this guide, list the particular benefits hoped for by buying green power for the organization. Wherever possible, these benefits should be linked to the organization's environmental goals.

Financial Considerations

Cost is usually the primary concern with green power, so the procurement plan should make a point of discussing it. Several strategies are available to help minimize and manage the extra cost of green power:

- Buy green power for only part of the organization's energy use. Green power does not have to be used for all energy needs. For example, the organization might buy green power for just 5 or 10 percent of its electricity use. Buying 5 percent green power may add less than 2 percent to the organization's electricity bill. Alternatively, some renewable electricity products cost less because they already are blended with conventional electricity.
- Make a longer-term purchase. Consider the contract's length in conjunction with the quantity and cost of power purchased. A short-term contract (typically less than three years) may offer greater flexibility in the future but also may cost more. But a longer contract can reduce the risk to the supplier, allowing it to offer a lower price than under a shorter contract. The right contract length is based on the particular situation and products available.
- Seek a fixed-price contract. Because its cost of fuel is predictable, renewable energy is often available at a fixed price without any fuel-cost adjustments. Check with the supplier, particularly if the organization is considering a utility green-pricing

program, to see whether green power customers are exempted from fuel-cost adjustments.
- Offset the cost with savings from energy efficiency. Reducing the total amount of electricity purchased helps make green power more affordable. When reviewing green power providers, organizations may find that some providers also offer energy efficiency services, with the goal of no net increase in their customers' power bills.
-

> Reducing the cost of green power
>
> In 2003, the University of Pennsylvania doubled its already large purchase of green power to 40 million kWh. In addition to doubling its purchase, Penn extended its earlier commitment term from 3 years to 10 years. Both of these factors may have reduced the price they pay for green power. Penn also has paid for its significant commitment through savings from aggressive energy conservation. For example, over the past few years, Penn has reduced its peak electric demand by 18%.

- Use savings from competitive choices. Competitive choices of either green power or commodity electricity may lead to savings on energy costs, which can be used to buy green power. Or the extra cost of green power can be limited to the amount of savings from competition. Be aware that switching to less expensive conventional power can also mean dirtier power, so ask the electricity supplier for information about the emissions from its product, and make sure those emissions do not cancel out the benefits of the green power bought with the savings.
- Specify a price cap or maximum total budget. Specify the maximum price per kilowatt-hour or the total cost, or simply place a cap on the renewable portion of the purchase. A drawback of this approach is that suppliers are likely to bid at or near the specified price cap. But if the organization is interested mainly in other aspects of green power, such as environmental benefits or hedge value, this can be a good approach. Even if a price cap is not the most important consideration, it is a good idea to decide on the highest price

the organization is willing to pay for green power, as part of its internal procurement planning.
- Use incentives for buying green power. A few states offer incentives that reduce the cost of green power. In almost all cases, these incentives are paid directly to the power marketer, so the incentive will already be factored into the price quoted and does not need to be requested separately. The power marketers and the state's energy department will know about any green power-purchasing incentives that are paid directly to the purchaser. For more information about available incentives, visit the Database of State Incentives for Renewable Energy at www.dsireusa.org.

Even with these cost reduction techniques, green power often is more expensive than standard power. To justify this extra expense, it is important to consider the benefits of green power. After weighing all the benefits, many organizations decide that green power is an inexpensive way to help achieve various organizational goals.

Procurement Methods

The best way to buy power depends on the green power options available to the organization as well as its procurement rules. Generally, the greater the load that the organization can bundle together in one purchase, the more attractive it will be to a supplier.

The following explains typical ways to buy green power. Federal agencies must work within the procurement rules applicable to the federal government, which are explained further in appendix A.

- *Negotiate with the utility.* Buying power is simple, though the choices are fewer, if the organization is served by a utility in a regulated market with only one supplier. If the local utility offers green power, the organization can collect information by visiting the utility's Web site and calling to discuss its interest. Perhaps the only issue is the quantity the organization wants to buy, but it may be able to negotiate a slight price break if it is making a large purchase. If the utility does not offer green power and the organization is a large, highly visible customer, it may be able to encourage the utility to offer green power by promising to buy a large amount.

Likewise, the organization may be able to persuade the utility to seek third-party certification if its product is not currently certified.
- *Call several sellers.* An organization can keep the procurement process relatively simple by calling the few green power providers active in its area. An off-theshelf product may meet its needs. If the organization wants something different and only one or two green power suppliers are in the area, it can call them to discuss the options and let them know the organization would be interested in a proposal. After a discussion, the organization may be ready to negotiate directly with one of the suppliers about product definition, certification, price, and terms. Or if the organization is planning a large purchase, the suppliers may be willing to tailor something to its needs.
- *Request proposals.* Large companies, and public institutions in particular, often issue a formal solicitation or request for proposals (RFP). An RFP requires more time and effort for preparation, evaluation, and negotiation, but it may be more suitable for a large purchase and when many green power options are available. With an RFP, it is important to understand the organization's own objectives and communicate them clearly in the solicitation. Third-party certification and verification can be specified in the RFP evaluation criteria.

RFPs can be as simple as a letter sent to selected suppliers, describing the organization's objectives and asking for a bid. This would be appropriate if just a few suppliers are available. RFPs can also be more formal, casting a wider net through a broadly advertised solicitation. This requires more effort to prepare and evaluate responses. Government agencies must follow the procurement rules governing their agency.

A two-step process is possible, too, in which the organization first issues a request for qualifications (RFQ) and, based on the responses, sends a more detailed RFP to those suppliers that meet its general qualifications. The RFQ would be broadcast to a larger audience, not only to find out who meets the organization's qualifications, but also to gauge the amount of interest.

For large purchases, RFPs may be addressed to renewable power generators (wholesale) as well as retail suppliers. Buying directly from generators may lower the cost but probably will require a longer-term purchase commitment. The Green Power Partnership offers assistance to partners putting together a green power purchase RFP; FEMP provides the same service for federal agencies. For RECs, the World Resources Institute provides guidelines and a sample contract for an RFP (www.thegreenpower-group.org/credits.html).

RFP procurement

The State of New Jersey is buying 10% of its energy load (54 million kWh/year) from new wind facilities in Pennsylvania. This purchase is consistent with a number of state environmental policies, but was complex because of the many agencies involved and tight state budgets. To find a supplier, New Jersey issued an RFP that gave greater weight to Greene certified products and lower emissions, resulting in a wind-only purchase.

Special Considerations for RECs

Certificates can be bought from REC marketers or sometimes directly from renewable energy generators. Several environmental brokers are active in REC markets, offering another approach to procurement that is increasingly being used by large purchasers. Brokers do not own the certificates but rely on their knowledge of the market to connect buyers and sellers for a small fee. They can help negotiate deals that take into account an organization's unique interests.

Several issues need to be addressed when buying certificates. The attributes that the certificate represents should be clearly stated in a contract. If the organization plans to claim credit for these attributes, the contract should express in writing that the purchaser will receive title to them. If attributes like a reduction in carbon emissions have been sold separately to another party, then the exceptions should be clearly stated. The organization should make sure that the attributes it buys have not been double-sold and claimed by another party. Green-e certification can help ensure that the benefits promised by the supplier are actually realized. In addition, RECs have separate markets, depending on whether the certificates will be used to comply with the state's renewable policy requirements or for voluntary reasons. Prices in voluntary markets are generally well below those in compliance markets.

An organization may want to buy certificates only from renewable energy generators or marketers that meet its specifications, so the same selection criteria mentioned earlier in this chapter should still be considered in the procurement process. In fact, because certificates can come from any geographic area, the location where the certificate was generated, and therefore where the environmental benefits are likely to accrue, can be an important factor to consider.

7. Planning an on-Site Renewable Generation Project

Depending on the size of the system, on-site power projects tend to take more steps than do power purchases because they require more external coordination with the organization's utility, local governments, and contractors. For this reason, it is helpful to enlist outside technical expertise and not underestimate the length of time needed for a project like this. The following steps, along with the resources listed in chapter 10, can help. In the end, the renewable system will generate power and other benefits for many years to come.

Screening the Technologies

Based on work done in the first steps (chapter 5), the organization should have a good idea of its energy needs and the renewable resources available at its site. The next step is to perform a screening analysis to find those options best suited to the site. This screening should evaluate the options being considered, comparing the cost-effectiveness of the organization's current energy situation with that of a renewable power system. This screening should be based on the financial assessment methods that the organization would normally use for any capital investment, such as life-cycle cost, rate of return, and simple payback. The analysis should account for state and federal financial incentives, interconnection rules (e.g., insurance requirements or standby charges), and net- metering laws that may apply to the facilities. The result of this screening will be a specific technology that meets the organization's energy needs.

For on-site renewable power, bundling energy efficiency with renewable power is a common practice. The organization's site-specific situation (e.g., whether the generation system is connected to a grid, the facility's load shape, the utility's rate structure) determines the appropriate efficiency measures to include. At this point, it is a good idea to consider whether energy efficiency projects should be implemented together with the renewable generation technologies being considered.

An economic analysis must consider the approximate size of the renewable power system that the organization hopes to install. The size can be driven by the load to be served by the system, the organization's capital budget, or physical constraints at the site (such as rooftop area for PV systems or the rate of biomass fuel production). One option is to install the system incrementally, purchasing what the organization can afford now and adding more capacity over time. The modular nature of PV technology makes it especially suited to this approach, although wind can also be installed in somewhat larger modules. A contractor or utility representative can help choose the right-size system. The organization can also use one of the software tools listed in chapter 10.

The economic analysis should also decide whether the on-site power system will be used to provide backup power during utility grid outages. If so, the system must be designed to disconnect from the utility grid when a power outage occurs. The organization also must decide whether the system will include energy storage or backup generation, in order to provide power when renewable resources are not available. This analysis will be affected as well by whether the renewable generation will be part of a combined heat and power system (applicable to systems involving fuel combustion, such as landfill gas and biomass).

Obtaining Resources and Assistance

If the organization chooses to own and operate an on-site power system, it has much to learn, but excellent information resources are available. Before making a purchase, the organization's project team should study the technology and understand what it wants and what questions to ask, in order to be able to write a procurement specification. At this point, it would be wise to call on outside experts who can help with the technical and financial aspects of a renewable power project. Technical assistance may be available through the local utility, the state energy office, energy service providers, energy service companies, consultants, manufacturers, and equipment vendors. In addition, FEMP offers technical assistance to federal agencies.

The financial details are usually what make or break a power project, so the project should collect information about incentives that could make the project more cost-effective. Some state programs may also require that only certified installers install systems. Many states offer financial incentives specifically for customers that install qualified renewable generation systems. These incentives may take the form of direct payments (rebates), competitive solicitations, consumer financing, or lower taxes (either sales or property tax). In addition, the federal government offers an investment tax credit for solar and geothermal energy systems, among other incentives for renewable energy. For more information, visit the Database of State Incentives for Renewable Energy at www.dsireusa.org. The state energy office, local utility, or renewable-energy equipment vendor will also have information about which incentive programs apply to its situation.

Utility rate impacts should also be investigated carefully. The organization should check with the local utility to see whether on-site generation would lower its demand charges or generate electricity at a time of day when prices are higher. Facilities with their own generation systems sometimes also qualify for reduced "self-generation" rates.

Using Incentives to Finance an On-Site Generation System

The City of Portland, Oregon used a variety of funding mechanisms to pay for a $1.3 million methane-powered fuel cell. Portland received a $200,000 grant from the U.S. DOE and a utility rebate of $247,000 (essentially returning a green power premium that the City had earlier paid). To finance the remainder, it entered into a lease-purchase arrangement with Western Bank, which was able to qualify for a $224,000 state tax credit because it owned the facility. Western Bank returned much of the tax credit to the City in the form of advantageous lease terms.

Creating a Project Plan

Once the organization has decided on a specific technology, it is time to conduct a detailed feasibility study. This study will quantify all the costs and benefits of the project to evaluate its cost-effectiveness. The study should be based on inputs that are as specific as possible to the organization's situation, such as quoted prices from vendors.

If the project appears feasible, the project team can then decide on a plan to have the renewable power system financed, built, and installed. Financing is a critical aspect of the project, and it should account for any federal and state incentives for which the organization's system is eligible. Make sure that the system is designed to meet the requirements of the incentive program.

In addition, some renewable resources, such as biomass, will probably require air permits from the local air resources control board. The project plan should account for the time and expense of acquiring these permits. As with any other type of facilities project, the team must secure the necessary land-use and building permits and variances required for the project. The team also will need to apply for interconnection with the local electric utility (for grid-connected systems), which can be a complex and time-consuming process.

Procurement Strategy

Purchases for on-site generation differ from power purchases. In many cases, an organization may buy, own and operate its own generation equipment. In some circumstances, though, it can enter into a power purchase agreement to buy the electricity generated by a renewable energy system installed on its property without actually owning the system. This approach may not be widely available in states that allow electricity to be purchased only from a qualified utility.

The procurement options for on-site generation generally fall into the following categories:

- *Act as the general contractor.* If the organization has design engineers on staff, they can draw up the specifications and then solicit bids for equipment and installation. This arrangement works well if the organization wants to do some of the work in-house. Keep in mind, however, that if the organization has no

experience with renewable energy systems, it runs the risk of ending up with a poorly performing system.
- *Hire a general contractor for a turnkey system.* An organization probably will use an RFP to select an equipment manufacturer, a system designer, or a system installer to help design the system to its needs, to buy the materials, to arrange for installation, and to commission the system. Note that some companies (particularly in the PV industry) are vertically integrated, from manufacturing, to design and installation, to operations and maintenance.
- *Hire an energy services company (ESCO).* The ESCO will be responsible for design, installation, maintenance, and financing. This differs from a turnkey project in that ESCOs typically work under performance contracts, meaning that they are paid according to how well the project is carried out. Usually this is through energy savings, but success can also be based on the amount of power generated or the system's reliability. ESCOs also often provide at least part of the project financing, which can be very helpful for organizations— such as government agencies—with very limited capital budgets. Usually, ESCO projects need to be large, or part of a larger contract, in order to justify the transaction costs.
- *Buy power from an independently owned system.* When considering on-site green power, some companies decide not to install solar PV systems because of the high capital investment, maintenance costs, and financial returns that fall short of company standards. To overcome these barriers, an organization can host an on-site generation system and agree to buy the power without actually owning the equipment. This approach is known as a *services model,* and it can greatly simplify the process of installing on-site renewable power. As with other types of green power purchases, make sure that the contract also transfers the environmental and other benefits of the green power, in order to claim full credit for the organization's purchase.

> ### Procuring On-Site Generation
> ### through a Services Model
>
> In 2004, Staples initiated a solar services project for its location in Rialto, CA. The project developer, SunEdison, Inc., arranged for financing, design and construction of a 260 kW solar array. In return, Staples signed a 10-year power purchase agreement (PPA) with SunEdison, with the option to renew for 5-year intervals. The solar PV system will provide benefits of peak load shaving and reduced GHG emissions. Further, Staples will avoid all capital and maintenance costs. The price for power in the contract is competitive with local commercial rates, and the PPA has a fixed cost structure that acts to hedge against price volatility in retail electricity.

Choosing a Vendor

When choosing a vendor, it generally is a good idea to get more than one bid, so the first step is to find several possible vendors for a given project. The Web sites for the major trade groups in this area—the Solar Energy Industries Association and the American Wind Energy Association—offer information about their members' expertise and interests, and chapter 10 lists more sources.

When choosing a vendor, the organization should obtain comparative information from the companies it is considering, usually through either a request for qualifications (RFQ) or a request for proposals (RFP). An RFP is appropriate if the organization already has a detailed system design and simply wants a vendor to implement that design. An RFQ is better for comparing vendors' qualifications and experience, to select one to both design and implement the system. Because the design of on-site renewable systems tends to be site specific and because design details are often resolved differently by different vendors, the RFQ approach often leads to the system best tailored to the organization's needs.

Some factors to consider when choosing a provider of on-site generation are the following:

- *Experience.* The vendor's experience and familiarity with the type of system the organization is considering is extremely important. Also determine the vendor's experience with interconnection issues (if the system will be connected to the

grid). A quick way to judge a vendor's experience is the length of time it has been in business and the number of similar systems it has installed.
- *Performance history.* It is very important to check references from previous customers, preferably for systems similar to the one the organization is considering. Another important factor is whether there are any judgments or liens against the vendor, which would indicate problems with previous projects.
- *Licenses and certification.* To be eligible for state incentives, some states require that the system be installed by a licensed contractor, whereas other states certify installers that have received the relevant training. As with any other capital project, licenses and certification are an indicator of a contractor's qualifications.
- *Liability and professional insurance.* If any problems arise with the system during installation or operation, it is important that the contractor have adequate insurance to protect the purchasing organization from liability. The contractor should also be responsible for any problems with interconnecting to the grid.

Anticipating Possible Barriers

When implementing a renewable generation project, the organization must work with various entities to obtain permits, connect to the utility system, and perform other activities external to the facility. Some of these steps will end up requiring more time, effort, or money than originally anticipated and may pose barriers that must be overcome.

Generally these barriers fall into two categories: technical and regulatory. Most technical barriers pertain to the local utility's electrical interconnection requirements. Other technical barriers are fuel availability and storage; space limitations; power-quality impacts; fire, safety, and zoning requirements; and operations and maintenance issues. Regulatory barriers pertain mainly to the required permits and approvals, such as air emissions permits, utility standby charges, exit fees, regional transmission charges, and land-use permits.

Often the contractor for the project can be made responsible for overcoming these barriers as they arise. If this seems like a good option, the project team should explore it with the contractor when writing the RFP and reviewing the proposals. The FEMP guide to distributed energy resources offers many tips for resolving any problems that may arise when implementing a renewable power project.

Installing and Operating an on-Site Renewable Generation System

Once the organization's on-site generation system has been designed, it is time to put the contracts in place and begin construction. As with any capital project, it is important to stay involved during the construction to resolve any problems that might arise.

When the construction has been completed, the project team should monitor and verify the system's energy performance. Does everything work as planned? What is the system's actual energy production? If it is not as estimated, what can be done to improve the system's performance? Information about system performance is useful in communicating the benefits of the project to internal and external audiences.

Measurement and validation generally proceed in two steps. The first is the postconstruction evaluation (or commissioning), in which a contractor's work is inspected and the system is tested to make sure that it meets regulatory and design specifications. The second step is monitoring and verifying the system's performance over a longer period, such as the first year of operation (although continuous monitoring is necessary to catch any performance problems that arise). It is important to plan for this stage at the early phases of the project, in order to design a useful data acquisition system.

Finally, all renewable power systems require periodic maintenance in order to perform as intended. The organization must decide whether its staff has the expertise and time to do this or whether it should contract with the equipment vendor or a service company to maintain the system.

8. CAPTURING THE BENEFITS OF THE PURCHASE

After buying or installing green power, the organization should consider various promotional strategies and marketing to generate measurable, positive publicity and public relations benefits. To maximize the positive publicity, both inside and outside the organization, the purchase of green power should be made part of the organization's comprehensive environmental management efforts. The organization's achievements should be significant and well documented so that claims made to the public are credible.

On-Site Photovoltaic System

Johnson and Johnson's corporate environmental goals include a goal to reduce its energy-related emissions of carbon dioxide. To help meet these goals, the company opted to purchase renewable power, specifically an on-site solar photovoltaic (PV) system at its Janssen Pharmaceutica facility in Titusville, New Jersey. A state rebate eventually paid for 57% of project costs, and additional federal incentives will allow for accelerated depreciation of the equipment. Even with these subsidies, the project did not rise to the company's minimum rate of return for capital expenditures. The solar PV project had support from senior management, though, because of its positive environmental benefits. This high-level support was vital to project approval. Based on initial data, the 500 kW system will generate about 500,000 kWh per year and can handle about 10% of the facility's load at peak times. Johnson and Johnson is evaluating numerous solar PV projects in addition to the three systems it currently owns.

The Environmental Benefits

When an organization highlights the benefits of its purchase of green power, it is important that it know the quantity of emissions avoided. These emissions can be greenhouse gases (GHGs), primarily carbon dioxide, as well as other significant pollutants that affect the environment and human health, such as sulfur dioxide, nitrogen oxides, and mercury. A buyer of green power can calculate its reduction of emissions and count them toward an environmental or energy goal. To help with these calculations, analysis tools are available from the EPA Green Power

Partnership (www.epa.gov/cleanenergy/powerprofiler.htm) and the World Resource Institute's Green Power Market Development Group (www.thegreenpowergroup.org/gpat/).

The concern about climate change, and GHGs in particular, has prompted many organizations to make a GHG emissions inventory. An inventory is a detailed list of emissions by source and type of greenhouse gas, usually expressed in metric tonnes of carbon dioxide equivalent (CO2e).

An inventory serves many purposes, including

- Identifying opportunities for reduction and managing GHGs.
- Participating in public reporting and voluntary reduction initiatives.
- Participating in mandatory government-reporting programs.
- Trading in GHG emissions markets.
- Providing recognition for early voluntary action.

Using an inventory to record changes in GHG emissions sets the foundation for companies, organizations, and others to benefit from buying green power in future climate change policy frameworks. An inventory also allows organizations to record their emissions information in an official registry with a government agency. Several GHG registry programs have been established to record GHG reductions, including the California Climate Action Registry, Wisconsin's Voluntary Emissions Reduction Registry, the U.S. Department of Energy's 1605b Voluntary Greenhouse Gas Reporting program, and the Regional Greenhouse Gas Registry being developed by the Northeast States for Coordinated Air Use Management.

For more information, see the GHG accounting standards developed by the GHG Protocol Initiative at www.ghgprotocol.org.

Internal Promotion

One of the benefits of buying green power is improving employees' morale. To capitalize on this, companies and organizations often choose to promote their purchase or installation internally using the following methods:

- *Include "energy news" in internal publications.* Internal publications, such as newsletters, are valuable ways of

communicating information to an organization's employees, stakeholders, and affiliates and also helps support the organization's mission, growth, and development.
- *Establish a staff adoption and recognition program.* Such a program encourages employees to buy green power through an organization-wide program. A staff adoption program should create incentives, provide information, set milestones for staff purchases over time, and recognize individual achievements.
-

External Promotion

Strategic external public relations maximize the positive publicity surrounding an organization's purchase of green power. In addition to the public relations benefits, the purchase can motivate additional purchases by the general public, the organization's customers, and its affiliates, thereby extending the impact of the initial purchase.

- *Construct a public relations plan.* Construct a plan to publicize to target audiences the organization's purchase or installation. The plan should include strategies for using existing distribution channels such as e-mail, Web sites, and direct mail to promote the organization and its commitment to renewable energy. An organization can create special print materials and press releases for distribution, and conduct e-mail campaigns that distinguish it as an innovative leader. Retail companies sometimes circulate special offers and coupons and even host events—such as renewable energy celebrations—at stores to attract new customers and communicate the benefits of the organization's green power purchase.
- *Use media contacts and press.* An organization may wish to write a press release describing its purchase, and circulate it to local and national media outlets. The organization can also research and contact local environmental writers and publications to encourage feature stories about the organization and its commitment to improve the environment.
- *Train staff to promote the organization's purchase.* Purchasers can instruct their staff about the details of the organization's purchase

and the best ways to highlight it to customers in daily sales interactions. Also teach them how to answer general questions about renewable energy.
- *Take advantage of all opportunities to promote the purchase.* Effective organizations use strategic business engagements and speaking events as well as existing interactions with the public to talk about the organization's environmental commitment and promote its purchase of green power. This may include marketing the organization's purchase on its products and encouraging its suppliers and affiliates to follow its lead and buy green power.

Using Green Power for Promotion and Branding

Hayward Lumber powers part of its manufacturing facility in Santa Maria, California with a 118 kW rooftop photovoltaic system. The PV system, which produces 45% of the facility's electric load, now serves as a brand name—Solar Truss—for the components that are produced at the plant. By branding their trusses, Hayward Lumber is educating contractors and architects that its trusses are built using renewable energy sources.

- *Work with third-party organizations.* Third-party organizations can help provide credibility to green power purchases that meet minimum purchasing benchmarks. These organizations also offer publicity channels that promote renewable energy and highlight environmental commitment. All the organizations sponsoring this guidebook help their partners and companies publicize their achievements in buying green power. Members of the EPA's Green Power Partnership and those who purchase Green-e certified products can also use these logos in their promotional activities.
- *Create marketing partnerships with green-power suppliers.* Offer retail customers the opportunity to sign up for green power, and reward them with benefits such as gift or discount cards, merchandise, or collateral products (e.g., T-shirts, hats) that tout the company's image as an environmental leader.

9. CONCLUSION

Purchasers of electricity can have a significant impact on the way that power is produced, both now and in the future. Businesses, governments, and nonprofits have an unprecedented and increasing range of options for buying green power. In those states that have restructured their electricity markets, retail access allows customers to choose their electricity supplier and, by extension, how their electricity is produced. In regulated markets, utility green-pricing programs enable customers to support the addition of renewable energy to the grid without leaving their current utility. Renewable energy certificates and on-site renewable generation allow organizations everywhere to achieve the benefits of green power. Organizations that act in their own—and society's—best interests can take advantage of the strategies outlined in this guidebook to help move the United States toward a more sustainable energy future.

10. RESOURCES FOR ADDITIONAL INFORMATION

U.S. Department of Energy

- Federal Energy Management Program (FEMP) www.eere.energy.gov/femp
- Green Power Network www.eere.energy.gov/greenpower
- FEMP Renewable Power Purchasing www.eere.energy.gov/femp/technologies/renewable_purchasepower.cfm
- World Resources Institute
- World Resources Institute home page www.wri.org
- GHG Protocol Initiative www.ghgprotocol.org
- Green Power Market Development Group www.thegreenpowergroup.org
- FEMP Distributed Power www.eere.energy.gov/femp/technologies/derchp.cfm

U.S. Environmental Protection Agency

- Clean Energy www.epa.gov/cleanenergy

- Green Power Partnership www.epa.gov/greenpower
- Energy Star www.energystar.gov
- Landfill Methane Outreach Program www.epa.gov/lmop
- EGRID database www.epa.gov/cleanenergy/egrid
- Power Profiler www.epa.gov/cleanenergy/powerprofiler.htm

Green-e Renewable Energy Certification Program

The Green-e Renewable Energy Certification Program is the nation's leading voluntary certification and verification program, designed to help businesses and households compare and select clean renewable energy options. Green-e sets consumer protection and environmental standards for energy products and verifies that Green-e certified products meet those standards. Energy products that meet the Green-e standards are identified by the Green-e logo.

Certification ensures the quality of renewable energy products. All Green-e-certified products meet stringent requirements for air emissions, energy from new renewable facilities, and truth in advertising. These strict standards are set through a collaborative process with environmentalists, consumer advocates, marketers, and energy experts. Green-e's annual verification process and marketing compliance review ensure that providers meet these standards. By requiring these consumer and environmental safeguards, Green-e builds consumer confidence in renewable energy products, which helps expand the market for high-quality products.

Green-e provides clear information about energy options to enable purchasers to make informed decisions. Green-e works with companies and organizations purchasing certified green power to highlight their purchase and educate consumers about the benefits of buying renewable energy. Green-e also conducts public education and outreach campaigns in regions across the nation to inform consumers about their options and build demand for renewable energy. The Green-e Web site, www.green-e.org, and toll-free number (888-63-GREEN) are widely used resources that allow consumers to compare certified products in any region and to select the superior green power option that meets their needs.

Green-e also identifies products manufactured by companies that buy certified green power, bringing renewable energy to the attention of millions of diverse consumers across the nation. Through Green-e's product labeling initiative, claims such as "Made with Certified Renewable Energy" and "We Buy Certified Renewable Energy" may now appear on consumer products, accompanied by the Green-e logo and Web site. These labels appear on products in grocery stores, carpet labels, and even on bottles of wine in restaurants. The initiative advances renewable electricity use as a new type of environmental performance indicator for consumer products, similar to other consumer labels for recycled products, organic food, fair trade practices, and energy efficiency.

Green-e is a program of the Center for Resource Solutions. For more information, visit www.green-e.org or www.resource-solutions.org.

ADDITIONAL RESOURCES

Overview

Developing a strategic energy management plan:
ENERGY STAR for business: www.energystar.gov, follow the links to "Business Improvement" then "Guidelines for Energy Management".
Electricity restructuring:
FEMP's restructuring Web site: pnnl-utilityrestructuring.pnl.gov.
Current state of green power markets:
Bird, Lori, and Blair Swezey. 2003. *Estimates of Renewable Energy Developed to Serve Green Power Markets in the United States*. Golden, CO: National Renewable Energy Laboratory, February (www.eere.energy.gov/ greenpower/ resources/tables/new_gp_cap.shtml).

Benefits of Green Power

Public support for renewable energy:
Farhar, Barbara C., and Ashley H. Houston. 1996. *Willingness to Pay for Electricity from Renewable Energy.* Golden, CO: National Renewable Energy Laboratory, September.
Motivations for purchasing green power:
Holt, E., R.Wiser, M. Fowlie, R. Mayer, and S. Innes.
2000. *Understanding Non-Residential Demand for Green Power.* Prepared for the American Wind Energy Association and the National Wind Coordinating Committee (www.nationalwind.org/pubs).
Economic development and job creation:

National Wind Coordinating Committee. 2003. *Assessing the Economic Development Impacts of Wind Power.* March (www.nationalwind.org/pubs).

Environmental Law and Policy Center. *Job Jolt: The Economic Impacts of Repowering the Midwest: The Clean Energy Development Plan for the Heartland* (www.repowermidwest.org/Job%20Jolt/JJfinal.pdf).

Environmental benefits:

Serchuck, Adam. 2000. *The Environmental Imperative for Renewable Energy: An Update.* College Park, MD: Renewable Energy Policy Project (REPP), University of Maryland. April (www.repp.org/repp_pubs/articles/envImp/envImp.pdf).

EPA's Global Warming Web site: www.epa.gov/globalwarming.

Emissions credits:

Wooley, David R. 2000. *A Guide to the Clean Air Act for the Renewable Energy Community.* College Park, MD: Renewable Energy Policy Project (REPP), University of Maryland.

Issue Brief no. 15. February (www.repp.org/repp_pubs/articles/issuebr15/caaRen.pdf).

National Wind Coordinating Committee. 2002. *Credit Trading and Wind Power: Issues and Opportunities.* May (www.nationalwind.org/pubs/).

Renewable Energy Certificates (RECs)

Hamrin, Jan, and Meredith Wingate. 2003. *Regulator's Handbook on Tradable Renewable Certificates.* San Francisco: Center for Resource Solutions. May (www.resource-solutions.org/RegulatorHandbook.htm).

EPA's Green Power Locator: provides links to retail and wholesale marketers of renewable energy certificates: www.epa.gov/greenpower/locator.htm.

The Green Power Network lists brokers and wholesale marketers: www.eere.energy.gov/greenpower/markets/ certificates.shtml.

Green-e lists certificate marketers and brokers that offer certified products: www.green-e.org.

The World Resources Institute offers a sample REC contract: www.thegreenpowergroup.org/ Sample_REC_Contract.doc.

Hanson, Craig, and Vince Van Son. 2003. *Renewable Energy Certificates: An Attractive Means for Corporate Customers to Purchase Renewable Energy.* Washington, DC: World Resources Institute

(www.thegreenpowergroup.org/Installment5.pdf).

Utility Green-Pricing Programs

Holt, Edward, and Meredith Holt. 2004. *Green Pricing Resource Guide.* 2nd ed. Washington, DC: American Wind Energy Association.

Lieberman, Dan. 2002. *Green Pricing at Public Utilities: A How-to Guide Based on Lessons Learned to Date.* Center for Resource Solutions and Public Renewables Partnership. October. (www.resource-solutions.org/PRP.htm).

Green Power Product Lists

The Green Power Network maintains lists of products offered in each state: www.eere.energy.gov/greenpower.

The EPA Green Power Partnership supports a Green Power Locator: www.epa.gov/greenpower/locator.htm.

Green-e maintains a list of certified products offered in each state: www.green-e.org/your_e_choices/pyp.html.

On-Site Renewable Generation

FEMP. 2002. *Using Distributed Energy Resources:*
A How-to Guide for Federal Facility Managers. Washington, DC: U.S. Department of Energy, Federal Energy
Management Program. DOE/GO-102002-1520. May (www.eere.energy.gov/femp/technologies/ derchp_resources.cfm).

Massachusetts DOER. 2001. *Renewable Energy and Distributed Generation Guidebook: A Developer's Guide to Regulations, Policies and Programs That Affect Renewable Energy and Distributed Generation Facilities in Massachusetts.*

Massachusetts Division of Energy Resources. April (www.state.ma.us/doer/pub_info/guidebook.pdf).

California Energy Commission: www.energy.ca.gov/renewables/index.html.

Pennsylvania Department of Environmental Protection. 2003. *Small Wind Electric Systems: A Pennsylvania Consumer's Guide*
(www.dep.state.pa.us/dep/deputate/pollprev/energy/wind/small_wind_pa.pdf).

New York State Energy Research and Development Agency: www.nyserda.org/energyresources/photovoltaics.html

and www.nyserda.org/energyresources/wind.html.

Government Incentives for Renewable Energy

The Database of State Incentives for Renewable Energy includes information about capital cost incentives as well as net-metering laws: www.dsireusa.org.

Clean Energy States Alliance: www.cleanenergystates.org.

The American Wind Energy Association lists states' incentives for small wind installations: www.awea.org, follow links to "Small Wind Systems" then "State by State Information".

Bolinger, Mark, Ryan Wiser, Lew Milford, Michael Stoddard, and Kevin Porter. 2001. *Clean Energy Funds: An Overview of State Support for Renewable Energy.* Berkeley, CA: Lawrence Berkeley National Laboratory. LBNL-47705. April (http://eetd.lbl.gov/ea/EMS/reports/47705.pdf).

Interconnection with the Utility Grid

In 2003 the Federal Energy Regulatory Commission (FERC) issued standard procedures and a standard interconnection agreement for the interconnection of generators larger than 20 megawatts. FERC also proposed a rule to apply to the interconnection of small generators no larger than 20 megawatts: www.ferc.gov/industries/electric/indus-act/gi.asp.

California Rule 21: standards for interconnection of distributed energy resources: www.energy.ca.gov/distgen/interconnection/ california_requirements. html.

Standards Board of the Institute for Electrical and Electronics Engineers, Inc. (IEEE). Standard 1547: "Standard for Interconnecting Distributed Resources with Electric Power Systems": grouper.ieee.org/groups/scc21/dr_shared.

DOE Distributed Power program: www.eere.energy.gov/distributedpower

FEMP Interconnection and Permitting Guide: www.eere.energy.gov/femp/ technologies/ derchp_ipg.cfm.

Larsen, C., B. Brooks, and T. Starrs. 2000. *Connecting to the Grid: A Guide to PV Interconnection Issues.* 3rd ed. Interstate Renewable Energy Council (http://irecusa.org/connect/library.html).

Measurement and Verification of System Performance

FEMP. 2000. *M and V Guidelines: Measurement and Verification for Federal Energy Management Projects, version 2.2.* Section VIII of these guidelines covers renewable energy projects. (www.eere.energy.gov/femp/financing/ superespcs _measguide.cfm).

PVWATTS is a calculator to estimate the output from photovoltaic solar installations. The model calculates monthly and annual energy production in kilowatt-hours and monthly savings in dollars.

See http://rredc.nrel.gov/solar/calculators/PVWATTS.

For more information about PV systems, see: American Solar Energy Society: www.ases.org.

Solar Electric Power Association: www.solarelectricpower.org. Solar Energy Industries Association: www.seia.org.

North Carolina Solar Center: www.ncsc.ncsu.edu.

California Energy Commission. 2000. *Buying a Photovoltaic Solar Electric System: A Consumer Guide.* April (www.energy.ca.gov/reports/500-99-008.PDF).

California Energy Commission. 2001. *A Guide to Photovoltaic (PV) System Design and Installation.* June (www.energy.ca.gov/reports/
2001 -09-04_500-01 -020.PDF).

Renewable energy trade associations: American Bioenergy Association: www.biomass.org. American Solar Energy Society: ww.ases. org. American Wind Energy Association: www.awea.org. Biomass Energy Research Association: www.bera1.org. Geothermal Energy Association: www.geo-energy.org. Geothermal Resources Council: www.geothermal.org. Interstate Renewable Energy Council: www.irecusa.org.

Low Impact Hydropower Institute: www.lowimpacthydro.org.

National Hydropower Association: www.hydro.org.

Solar Electric Power Association: www.solarelectricpower.org.

Solar Energy Industries Association: www.seia.org. Utility Wind Interest Group: www.uwig.org. Windustry: www.windustry.com.

On-site renewable generation financial analysis tools:

Each of the many available tools offers different features, which should be examined closely to determine whether they are appropriate to the particular situation.

ProForm

Developer: Lawrence Berkeley National Laboratory

Allows an integrated environmental and financial prefeasibility analysis of on-site renewable energy and energy efficiency projects. ttp://poet.lbl.gov/Proform

RETscreen International

Developer: Natural Resources Canada's CANMET Energy Diversification Research Laboratory (CEDRL)

Assesses the economics of various renewable energy installations. www.retscreen.net

RETFinance

Developer: Energy Analysis Team at NREL

Simulates a 30-year nominal dollar cash flow for renewable projects, including earnings, debt payments, levelized cost-ofelectricity, after-tax internal rate of return, and debt service coverage ratio (net operating income divided by total debt service). http://analysis.nrel.gov/retfinance

Clean Power Estimator

Developer: Clean Power Research

Offers a quick cost-benefit analysis for photovoltaics, solar thermal, wind, and energy efficiency for both residential and commercial buildings. www.clean-power.com/software.ht.

A version for California facilities is offered by the CEC. www.consumerenergycenter.org/renewable/estimator.

Federal Renewable Energy Screening Application (FRESA) Developer: U.S. Department of Energy, Energy Efficiency and Renewable Energy

Compares opportunities for renewables and conservation at federal facilities.

www.eere.energy.gov/femp/information/ download_software.cfm

Hybrid Optimization Model for Electric Renewables (HOMER)

Developer: NREL

Compares the cost-effectiveness of off-grid renewables with grid extensions or stand-alone generators. www.nrel.gov/homer.

Real Options Analysis Center

Developer: NREL

Provides online models for the valuation of renewable energy R and D and the valuation of distributed generation assets. www.nrel.gov/realoptions

FATE-2P (Financial Analysis Tool for Electric Energy Project)

Developer: NREL

A power plant project finance model for calculating the cost of energy or the internal rate of return for alternative energy projects.

Greenhouse Gas Resources

Hanson, Craig, and Janet Ranganathan. 2003. *Corporate Greenhouse Gas Emissions Inventories: Accounting for the Climate Benefits of Green Power.* Washington, DC: World Resources Institute
(www.thegreenpowergroup.org/Installment3.pdf).

U.S. Department of Energy's voluntary GHG registry: www.eia.doe.gov/oiaf/1605/frntvrgg.html.

U.S. Environmental Protection Agency's Climate Leaders, a voluntary government-industry partnership:
www.epa.gov/climateleaders.

World Wildlife Fund's (WWF) Climate Savers: www.world wildlife. org/climate/projects/
climate_savers.cfm.

Climate Neutral Network:
www.climateneu tral.com.

States that have or are developing climate registries:

The California Energy Commission has summarized state activities related to greenhouse gas inventories
www.energy.ca.gov/global_climate_change/
summary.html.

The California Climate Action Registry: www.climateregistry.org.

Wisconsin Voluntary Emission Reductions Registry Advisory Committee: www.dnr.state.wi.us/org/aw/air/hot/climchgcom/.

New Hampshire: www.des.state.nh.us/ard/climatechange/ghgr.htm

GLOSSARY

This glossary defines some of the important terms used in this guide. More definitions can be found at www.epa.gov/cleanenergy/glossary.htm.

Annual consumption. Annual consumption refers to the amount of electricity used by a consumer in one year and is typically measured in kilowatt-hours (kWh). This information can be acquired from your electricity bill or by contacting your energy provider.

Carbon dioxide. Burning fossil fuels releases into the atmosphere carbon that has been stored underground for millions of years. During the combustion process, the carbon in these fossil fuels is transformed into carbon dioxide, the predominant gas contributing to the greenhouse effect. Increases in the emissions of carbon dioxide and other gases, such as methane, due to the burning of fossil fuels and other human endeavors, accelerate heat-trapping processes in the atmosphere, gradually raising average temperatures worldwide. Carbon dioxide is absorbed and released at nearly equal rates by natural processes on the earth, an equilibrium that is disrupted when large amounts of carbon dioxide are released into the atmosphere by human activities, such as the burning of fossil fuels.

Combined heat and power (CHP). Combined heat and power (CHP) is an electricity generation technology, also known as *cogeneration*, that recovers waste heat from the electric generation process to produce simultaneously other forms of useful energy, such as usable heat or steam. On average, two-thirds of the input energy used to make electricity is lost as waste heat. In contrast, CHP systems are capable of converting more than 70 percent of the fuel into usable energy.

Commodity electricity. Commodity electricity is generic electricity not associated with a particular power generation source.

Competitive markets. Until recently, most consumers received generation, transmission, and distribution services from one local utility company. As a regulated monopoly, the utility was given an exclusive franchise to provide electricity to consumers in a particular community. Rates were set, and consumers had little choice but to pay the rate for their area. In recent years, however, many states have restructured their electricity industry and are now allowing consumers to choose from among competing electricity suppliers.

In states permitting retail competition, sellers of electricity obtain power by contracting with various generation sources and setting their own price. Consumers in these states have the opportunity to choose their energy provider and purchase products based on the price or type of power supplied to their home or business. Some consumers are exercising this choice and switching to accredited "green power" resources. In states that have not restructured their electricity markets, consumers interested in purchasing renewable energy now have the option to participate in green-pricing programs offered by their local utility.

Conventional power. Conventional power is power produced from nonrenewable fuels such as coal, oil, natural gas, and nuclear fuels. These fuels are a finite resource that cannot be replenished once they have been extracted and used.

Distributed generation. Distributed generation refers to small, modular, decentralized, grid-connected, or off-grid energy systems located in or near the place where energy is used.

Electricity supplier. As states restructure their electricity markets, more and more customers will be able to choose from a range of energy suppliers that market different types of power products, including green power from renewable energy. Restructured local utilities offer electricity products generated exclusively from renewable resources or, more frequently, electricity produced from a combination of fossil and renewable resources. In states without restructured electricity markets, local utilities may offer green-pricing programs, in which customers may elect to have their utility generate a portion of their power from renewable sources.

Energy efficiency. Energy efficiency refers to products or systems using less energy to do the same or a better job than conventional products or systems can. Energy efficiency saves energy, saves money on utility bills, and helps protect the environment by reducing the amount of electricity (and associated environmental impacts) that needs to be generated.

Fossil fuels. Fossil fuels are the United States' principal source of electricity. The popularity of these fuels is due largely to their low cost. Fossil fuels come in three main forms: coal, oil, and natural gas. All three were formed many hundreds of millions of years ago before the time of the dinosaurs, hence the name *fossil fuels.* Because fossil fuels are a finite resource and cannot be replenished once they have been extracted and burned, they are not considered renewable.

Global climate change. For most of human history, changes in the earth's climate resulted from natural causes that took place over thousands of years. But today, human activities are beginning to affect our climate in serious and immediate ways by rapidly adding greenhouse gases to the atmosphere. These gases trap heat close to the earth that would otherwise escape into space, intensifying a natural phenomenon called the *greenhouse effect.* Over the next century, scientists project that global temperatures will rise two to six degrees Fahrenheit as a result of rising concentrations of greenhouse gases. Scientists also believe that this rate of global warming will be unprecedented compared with that of the past 10,000 years. Global warming could result in a rise in sea levels, changes in patterns of precipitation, more variable weather, and many other consequences. These changes threaten our health, agriculture, water resources, forests, wildlife, and coastal areas. For more information on the science and impacts of global climate change, visit the EPA's Global Warming Web site (www.epa.gov/globalwarming).

Greenhouse effect. The greenhouse effect is produced as greenhouse gases allow incoming solar radiation to pass through the earth's atmosphere, while preventing part of the outgoing infrared radiation from the earth's surface and lower atmosphere from escaping into outer space. This process occurs naturally and has kept the earth's temperature about 59 degrees Fahrenheit warmer than it would otherwise be. Current life on the earth could not be sustained without the natural greenhouse effect.

Greenhouse gases (GHG). Gases in the earth's atmosphere produce the greenhouse effect. Changes in the concentration of certain greenhouse gases, due to human activities such as the burning of fossil fuels, increase the risk of global climate change. Greenhouse gases include water vapor, carbon dioxide, methane, nitrous oxide, halogenated fluorocarbons, ozone, perfluorinate carbons, and hydrofluorocarbons.

Green power. Electricity that is generated from renewable energy sources is often marketed as "green power," a term that implies a smaller environmental impact from electricity generation. The resources that qualify as green power vary depending on the state or organization. For more details, see chapter 2.

Green power marketers. Energy suppliers operating in states that permit retail competition in the electricity markets are usually referred to as *green power marketers*. This term can also include utilities that offer green power options under what are typically referred to as *green-pricing programs*.

Green power products. Green power products refer to electricity generated exclusively from renewable resources or from a combination of fossil and renewable resources.

Green pricing. Green pricing is an optional service offered by regulated utilities to allow customers to support a greater level of utility investment in renewable energy by paying a premium on their electric bill. Usually green pricing is offered in areas that do not allow retail competition.

Interval meter. An interval meter is an electricity meter that measures a facility's energy usage in short increments (typically 15 minutes). These meters are useful for determining electricity demand patterns and participating in real-time pricing programs.

Kilowatt-hour (kWh). A kilowatt-hour is the basic unit for measuring the generation and consumption of electrical energy. A *megawatt-hour (MWh)* of electricity is equal to 1,000 kilowatt-hours. A *kilowatt* and a *megawatt* are units of generation capacity.

Low-impact hydropower. Low-impact hydropower is hydroelectric power generated with fewer environmental impacts, by meeting criteria such as minimum river flows, water quality, fish passage, and watershed protection. These hydropower facilities often operate in a "run of the river" mode, in which little or no water is stored in a reservoir.

Net metering. Net metering is a method of crediting customers for electricity that they generate on-site. Customers generating their own electricity offset what they would have purchased from their utility. If they generate more than they use in a billing period, their electric meter turns backward to indicate their net excess generation. Depending on the individual state or utility rules, the net excess generation may be credited to their account (in many cases at the retail price), carried over to a future billing period, or ignored.

New renewable generation. New renewable generation facilities are those built in the recent past or will be built to meet the growing market demand for green power. For Green-e certification, new generation must have come online since the late 1990s (depending on the region; see the Green-e Web site for more details).

On-site renewable generation. On-site renewable generation refers to electricity generated by renewable resources using a system or device located at the site where the power is used.

Peak demand. Peak demand is the maximum power consumption for a facility, measured over a short time period such as 15 minutes or an hour.

Power marketer. A power marketer is an entity that buys and sells power generated by others. A green power marketer is an electricity supplier that offers a green power product.

Renewable electricity. Renewable electricity is power generated from renewable resources and delivered through the power grid to end users.

Renewable energy certificate (REC). A renewable energy certificate (REC), also known as a *green tag* or *tradable renewable certificate,* represents the environmental, social, and other positive attributes of power generated by renewable resources. For example, RECs may represent the emissions avoided by renewable power generation compared with those of conventional sources. RECs can be purchased separately from electricity service.

Renewable energy resources. Renewable energy sources, such as wind, solar, geothermal, hydropower, and various forms of biomass, are continuously replenished on the earth. Some definitions also include municipal solid waste as a renewable resource.

Renewable portfolio standard (RPS). A renewable portfolio standard (RPS) is a regulatory mandate or target stating that a minimum percentage or amount of each electricity supplier's resource portfolio must come from renewable energy.

APPENDIX A. GREEN POWER CONSIDERATIONS FOR FEDERAL AGENCIES

Purchasing green power means making a difference by changing the way we select basic commodities. For the federal government, the largest consumer of electricity in the United States with an annual electricity bill of approximately $3.5 billion, the ability to make a difference is enormous. This appendix discusses considerations specific to federal agencies that buy green power.

When green power first became available, federal agencies were uncertain about what authority they could use to justify paying a premium for these products. Now, however, this uncertainty has largely been dispelled, for several reasons. First, Executive Order 13123 (see text box below) clarifies the federal government's interest in renewable energy by directing agencies to "strive to expand the use of renewable energy within its facilities and in its activities by . . . purchasing electricity from renewable energy sources." Second, as directed by Executive Order 13123, through a collaborative process, the Secretary of Energy set a goal for the federal government to meet the equivalent of 2.5 percent of its facilities' electricity consumption with new renewable energy sources by 2005.[1] Finally, the authority for purchasing renewable energy has been incorporated into the Federal Acquisition Regulations (FAR, subpart 23.2), carrying the force of law (see www.arnet.gov/far).

> Executive Order 13123
>
> Sec. 204. Renewable Energy. Each agency shall strive to expand the use of renewable energy within its facilities and in its activities by implementing renewable energy projects and by purchasing electricity from renewable energy sources.
>
> Sec. 301. Annual Budget Submission. Each agency's budget submission to OMB shall specifically request funding necessary to achieve the goals of this order.
>
> Sec. 404. Electricity Use. To advance the greenhouse gas and renewable energy goals of this order, and reduce source energy use, each agency shall strive to use electricity from clean, efficient, and renewable energy sources.
>
> Reduced Greenhouse Gas Intensity of Electric Power.. ..Agencies shall consider the greenhouse gas intensity of the source of the electricity and strive to minimize the greenhouse gas intensity of purchased electricity.
>
> Purchasing Electricity from Renewable Energy Sources.
>
> (1) Each agency shall evaluate its current use of electricity from renewable energy sources and report this level in its annual report to the President. Based on this review, each agency should adopt policies and pursue projects that increase the use of such electricity. Agencies should include provisions for the purchase of electricity from renewable energy sources as a component of their requests for bids whenever procuring electricity. Agencies may use savings from energy efficiency projects to pay additional incremental costs of electricity from renewable energy sources.
>
> Sec. 406(c) Retention of Savings and Rebates. Agencies granted statutory authority to retain a portion of savings generated from efficient energy and water management are encouraged to permit the retention of the savings at the facility or site where the savings occur to provide greater incentive for that facility and its site managers to undertake more energy management initiatives, invest in renewable energy systems, and purchase electricity from renewable energy sources.
>
> Sec. 605. Amendments to Federal Regulations. The Federal Acquisition Regulation and other Federal regulations shall be amended to reflect changes made by this order, including an amendment to facilitate agency purchases of electricity from renewable energy sources.

---

[1] New renewable energy covers any renewable energy acquired by the federal government after 1990 (www.eere.energy.gov/femp/technologies/ renewable_ fedrequire. cfm).

As a result of these developments, a number of agencies have successfully bought green power in most regions of the country. These purchases account for approximately 50 percent of the total federal renewable energy use, with the remainder consisting of on-site renewable power, thermal generation, and biofuels (summarized in table A-1). Considering all sources, as of July 2004 the federal government had fulfilled more than 80 percent of its 2005 renewable energy goal. By reading this guidebook and taking advantage of the technical support provided by the Department of Energy's (DOE) Federal Energy Management Program (FEMP), energy managers are taking an important step in helping the federal government achieve its renewable usage goals.

Agencies that are interested in participating in procurements run by the General Services Administration (GSA), the Defense Energy Support Center (DESC), or the Western Area Power Administration (Western) should read the section "Procurement Approaches to Renewable Electricity and Certificates" in this appendix.

Federal Definitions of Renewable Energy

In order to meet the federal 2005 renewable use goal, Executive Order 13123 (sec. 710) and FAR subpart 2.1 define renewable energy as "energy produced by solar, wind, geothermal, and biomass power." DOE's definition of biomass resources, as defined under the Biomass Research and Development Act of 2000, is "organic matter available on a renewable or recurring basis, including agricultural crops and trees, wood and wood wastes and residues, plants (including aquatic plants), grasses, residues, fibers, and animal wastes, municipal wastes, and other waste materials."

FEMP provides guidance on renewable resource definitions and other issues relating to Executive Order 13123's renewable use goal on its Web site (www.eere.energy.gov/femp/ technologies/renewable_energy. cfm). Note that FEMP guidance is subject to change.

Table A-1. Federal Renewable Technologies and Purchases, July 2004

Source	Annual Energy Contribution (GWh)
Biomass fuels	106
Biomass power	92
Biomass thermal	108
Green power purchases	668
Ground-source heat pump	179
Photovoltaics	28
Solar thermal	10
Wind	19
Total	1210

Source: DOE/FEMP.

Federal Motivations for Green Power Purchases

Owing to the large volume of electricity consumed by the federal government, even a slightly greater percentage of green power can have a large benefit for the environment and the overall green power market. In addition to the benefits discussed earlier in this guidebook, green power purchases by federal agencies provide benefits specific to federal customers.

Benefits accruing directly to a federal agency from a renewable energy purchase include

- *Compliance with federal goals.* Executive Order 13 123 and the resulting federal renewable energy directive have three energy management goals: energy efficiency, greenhouse gas reduction, and the use of renewable energy. Purchasing green power or installing on-site generation can help an agency meet all three of these goals.
- *Increased visibility.* Presidential awards are given to those agency energy management teams that strive to comply with Executive Order 13 1 23. Energy scorecards for each agency are tallied to gauge the degree of compliance. Members of the EPA's Green Power Partnership also are eligible for awards.
- *Accomplishment of an agency's organizational mission.* Many in the federal government understand the government's

overall mission to include a commitment to environmental protection. Beyond that general obligation, individual agencies, such as the EPA, have the specific mission of protecting the environment. Renewable energy purchases are one way to help fulfill both goals.
- *Demonstrate responsiveness and leadership.* The purchase of renewable energy represents a clear demonstration of the agency's responsiveness to its customers (or citizens), the majority of whom, according to several surveys, favor renewable energy. The federal government has shown that it can be a leader in the area of green power and renewable energy. Social benefits of federal purchases include the following:
- *National security.* National security is one of the principal responsibilities of the federal government. By purchasing domestically produced renewable energy, all federal agencies can contribute to the nation's energy security. Because of the special role of government facilities in national security, the use of distributed, on-site power generation resources at these facilities enhances the country's overall security.
- *Market transformation.* Given the size of the federal government's utility bill, significant purchases of green power by federal agencies would stimulate the overall green power market. A strong federal demand would demonstrate that switching to renewable energy was a national priority, would call attention to green power's societal and customer benefits, might increase the availability of renewable power products, and might help reduce their cost. The size of the federal government amplifies any benefits resulting from a purchase of green power.

Sources of and Limits to the Federal Authority to Purchase Green Power

Executive Order 13123

Executive Order 13123 provides the fundamental authority for federal agencies to buy green power. The goals of this order have been incorporated into the FAR.

FAR Part 23

FAR part 23 seeks to minimize the environmental impacts of federal purchases. Subpart 23.2 addresses energy and water efficiency and renewable energy and has been modified to incorporate much of Executive Order 13123. This subpart states, "The Government's policy is to acquire supplies and services that promote energy and water efficiency, advance the use of renewable energy products, and help foster markets for emerging technologies." Subpart 23.7 directs agencies to contract for environmentally preferable and energy-efficient products and services. "Environmentally preferable" is defined by FAR subpart 2.101 to mean "products or services that have a lesser or reduced effect on human health and the environment when compared with competing products or services that serve the same purpose. This comparison may consider raw materials acquisition, production, manufacturing, packaging, distribution, reuse, operation, maintenance, or disposal of the product or service."

Cost Minimization and Best Value

The FAR has traditionally focused on minimizing the government's costs by strongly favoring the procurement of the least expensive goods and services, often leaving contracting officers little room to consider value. Procurement reform during the 1990s, however, more closely aligned federal acquisition procedures with the commercial sector's practices through a stated preference for commercial products and the adoption of commercial business practices.

In addition, the traditional focus on least cost procurement has shifted to obtaining the best value (FAR part 1.102[a]). In determining best value, contracting officers can consider an array of factors besides cost, such as environmental and energy efficiency (FAR part 8.404[b][2]). As formally defined in the FAR (part 2.101), best value means "the expected outcome of an acquisition that, in the Government's estimation, provides the greatest overall benefit in response to the requirement."

Specification of Requirements

Part 11 of the FAR, "Describing Agency Needs," states that environmental objectives, including the purchase of products and services that use renewable energy technologies, must be considered when specifying requirements (FAR part 1 1.002[d]). Requirements for renewable energy should be specific enough to limit the number of factors in competing offers to be evaluated but general enough so as not to jeopardize the product's status as a "commercial item." In general, as the requirements become more specifically defined, the importance of price relative to other considerations increases (FAR part 15.101).

Commercial Items

In restructured electricity markets, the most direct path to a renewable energy purchase is to make use of the "commercial items" provisions in FAR part 12. Commercial items are broadly defined as goods and services sold competitively in the commercial marketplace in substantial quantities (FAR subpart 2.101). Since an active competitive market reduces procurement risks, agencies are strongly encouraged to favor the purchase of commercial items, through both specific language to that effect and the authorization to use less stringent acquisition procedures.

With large volumes being commercially traded in public markets each day, electricity is undisputed as a standard commercial item. But as a specific type of electricity, renewable energy's status as a commercial item is slightly less certain. Support for such a designation is aided by the ongoing development of active renewable energy exchanges in which commercial entities buy and sell renewable energy in large quantities.

Even in the absence of an active renewable energy market, agencies may specify a requirement for electricity (the standard commercial item) generated from renewable resources (a specification in addition to the standard commercial item). In most cases, the favorable contracting procedures afforded to commercial items would still be applicable. While the boundary between what is and is not considered a commercial item is often case specific, in general an agency should be wary of specifying any requirement beyond what is currently commercially available.

In addition, certification efforts by state and nongovernmental organizations are helping establish renewable energy as a commercial item by establishing a brand name. Third-party certification provides additional value to the federal government because of functions such as verification and annual audits to ensure no double counting. When buying green power for federal agencies, the GSA and DESC routinely use the commercial item designation and require third-party verification.

Innovative Purchase Opportunities

Even though the procurement of green power has become common enough that it is generally not "innovative," in some situations the methods just outlined do not apply, and so innovative methods are needed to implement a purchase. The Federal Acquisition Streamlining Act of 1994 and the Federal Acquisition Reform Act of 1996 encourage contracting officers to take initiative and pursue opportunities that they believe to be in the best interests of the government (FAR 1.102[d]).

Procurement Approaches to Renewable Electricity and Certificates

Restructured/Competitive Markets

In a competitive market, agencies must use competitive acquisition procedures to "shop" for renewable energy from a variety of providers. Since an agency will be evaluating competing offers, normal solicitation procedures must be followed. Federal agencies should follow one of two solicitation approaches: using designated contracting agencies, such as the GSA, the DESC, or, in some cases, Western; or serving as the contracting agency themselves. Although serving as the contracting agency offers more control and flexibility, the designated contracting agencies have gained significant expertise in the area of competitive electricity power procurement, including renewables.

Fully Regulated Markets

Where retail competition is not available, federal agencies may be able to buy green power through a green-pricing program offered by their local utility. If such a program exists, agencies should find out the specific enrollment or sign-up procedures. If a GSA areawide contract (AWC) is already in place with this utility, the agency should complete the utility's green-pricing contract, as well as the AWC Exhibit A contract. A competitive solicitation is not required, since it is a utility service.

Renewable Energy Certificates

Federal agencies can buy green power through renewable energy certificates throughout the country and in some foreign locations. Since a variety of suppliers offer RECs, normal solicitation procedures must be followed. Both GSA and DESC have experience with REC procurements.

Using GSA or DESC
GSA Power Procurement Services

GSA has assisted many federal agencies in the procurement of green power, and its ability to aggregate renewable requirements for many agencies may result in lower prices.

In restructured electricity markets, GSA helps identify federal facilities that use large amounts of electricity in a manner that is regarded favorably by the competitive energy service providers. For these customers, GSA seeks specific prices for those facilities and works with the facility managers to devise strategies that may result in lower long-term electricity prices in the restructured marketplace. Using these strategies, GSA has also made significant progress in making renewable energy available at competitive market prices for both renewable electricity and REC products. In addition, GSA is developing a variable-priced REC product that may provide additional financial value to purchasers.

One of the easier ways for federal agencies to buy green power is through the GSA's federal supply schedules (FSS), multiple award schedules. Green power and renewable energy have been added to the federal supply schedule under three different special item numbers (SINs). SIN 871-204 addresses "Managing the Procurement and Use of Electricity," which includes electricity from both renewable and nonrenewable sources. SIN 871-203 addresses "Managing the Procurement and Use of Natural Gas," which includes gas from both renewable and nonrenewable sources. SIN 871-299 covers

New Products/Services. The last supply schedule would be applicable to on-site generation resources that use renewably generated methane gas (such as landfill gas). Renewable energy certificates are also being added to the schedule under SIN 871-204 and SIN 871-299.

Supply schedules have several features that make them particularly well suited to serve the needs of those buying electricity in a restructured market:

- Multiple award schedules (MAS) list competing contractors offering comparable products and services. MAS contracts are awarded to all companies offering commercial items whose price has been determined by the GSA to be fair. The use of MAS is considered a competitive procedure under FAR 6.102[d][3].
- Maximum order limitations have been removed and replaced with maximum order thresholds, beyond which an agency is required to seek a price reduction from the contractor (FAR 8.404[3]).

- MAS contracts are priced on a most-favored commercial customer basis, and a price reduction clause requires the contractor to lower the agency's price in accordance with any corresponding price reductions to its most- favored commercial customer.

For the latest information on Federal Supply Schedules, go to www.gsa.gov/energyservices.

For details on the schedules just described, go to www.gsaelibrary.gsa.gov and search for the special item numbers listed above.

DESC Power Procurement Services

Under the DESC Electricity Program, solicitations may be issued for competitive power and/or RECs in states that have approved and implemented deregulation/restructuring and for RECs in states that have not implemented retail access.

DESC:

- Procures electricity for Department of Defense and federal civilian activities.
- Uses aggregation to attract market interest without customer cross-subsidization.
- Works with customers to identify risk preferences and risk-mitigation plans.
- Tailors each solicitation to market conditions and customer requirements.
- Conducts "best value" acquisitions.
- Competitively buys RECs in accordance with federal acquisition regulations.
- Contracts for Economic Load Response Services.
- Uses various pricing methods: fixed price, index, and Locational Marginal Pricing.
- Has more than six years of experience procuring power for the federal government.
- Performs contract administration functions.

DESC's program uses commercial practices for its solicitations and procurement strategy, which has been central to successfully engaging the market. In addition, DESC's program is flexible enough to support unusual and/or "out of the box" customer requests and requirements while complying fully with applicable procurement regulations. To view ongoing DESC solicitations or to find contact information for DESC's electricity acquisition team, go to www.desc.dla.mil.

Western Green Power Products

Western offers two types of renewable products to federal agencies. Facilities located in Western's 15-state western service territory can buy renewable electricity directly from Western even if they are not currently Western allocation customers. Regardless of location, federal agencies can purchase renewable energy certificates[1] from Western. For more information about these programs, see the Western's Web site at www.wapa.gov/powerm/pmrenpro.htm.

Agency Procurement

If an agency does not deem it advantageous to request assistance from the GSA, DESC, or Western, it may contract separately for electric service. In this case, the purchase should meet the requirements of FAR part 12 as described in the section "Commercial Items."

Federal Assistance for on-Site Renewable Generation Projects

On-site renewable generation projects face different issues than do power purchases, which may hinder their implementation. To help federal agencies tap the renewable resources that are available at their facilities, FEMP offers several programs to assist with on-site generation projects.

Renewable Resource Assessment

To help facility managers assess the quality of renewable energy resources at their location, FEMP is working with resource assessment

---

[1] These certificates are a type of REC but cannot be traded because they are available only to federal customers.

specialists to draw renewable resource maps for several different renewable energy technologies (available on FEMP's Web site).

The maps show where each renewable technology is cost-effective for federal facilities under differing assumptions about electricity prices and renewable system prices. For example, the maps for solar water heating indicate that at current electricity rates, more than 60 percent of the federal facilities in the nation could install a cost-effective solar system, whereas at electric utility rates of $0.10/kWh or more, solar water-heating systems would be cost-effective for almost any kind of federal facility.

Design Assistance and Training

FEMP can also help design renewable energy projects, especially those designated as Federal Energy Saver Showcases. This design assistance includes reviewing plans and specifications, developing product specifications, sizing systems, and drawing up guidelines for a project's costs. Some services are available on a for-fee basis.

FEMP also offers two renewable-energy training courses:

- "Implementing Renewable Energy Projects" is an overview of the technologies, covering costs and other factors to consider when selecting a system.
- "Design Strategies for Low-Energy, Sustainable, Secure Buildings" focuses on whole-building designs that inte- grate daylighting, energy-efficient equipment, and passive solar strategies for new federal buildings.

Funding Assistance

Financing can be a problem when appropriations for new projects are limited. Once a year, FEMP announces a "call for projects," in which federal agencies participate in a competitive selection process for technical assistance on their renewable energy projects. This funding is not for system purchases, but FEMP does help some project teams acquire additional project financing if needed.

In its annual Distributed Energy Resources (DER) call for projects, FEMP offers funds for technical assistance. Both on- grid and off-grid renewable energy systems qualify as DER technologies.

Agencies also may participate in FEMP's alternative financing programs, through which the contractor pays the up-front costs of an energy efficiency or renewable energy project and is repaid over the term of the contract from the agency's guaranteed energy cost savings. Agencies can obtain financing for biomass fuels, geothermal heat pumps, parabolic-trough solar collectors, and PV systems through these contracting vehicles.

Facilitated Projects

FEMP also encourages agencies to facilitate large projects that serve the needs of federal agency customers and that count toward the federal renewable energy goal. An example is a large renewable energy project on the tribal land of Native Americans served by the Bureau of Indian Affairs. Currently, the federal government has implemented 2 GWh of facilitated renewable energy projects, and about 740 GWh are pending.

Facilities in western states should contact the Bureau of Land Management (BLM) about opportunities to collaborate on a facilitated renewable energy project on federal land. FEMP and BLM recently identified those federal lands with the best potential for renewable energy projects (this study is available from FEMP's Web site). Because these projects are usually much larger than on-site projects, their contribution to the federal goal can be significant. However, facilitated projects do not require the direct federal purchase of renewables and therefore may be subject to different treatment in the future under the renewable purchase goals.

Key Elements of a Successful Procurement or on-site Installation

Based on several years of experience buying green power and installing on-site renewable energy systems, certain lessons for federal agencies have emerged.

Stakeholder Involvement

Green power advocates must get agreement in advance from stakeholders such as comptrollers, energy managers, and key decision makers. The stakeholders must participate in the decision process and make reasoned, balanced decisions. It is important to be honest and clear about the project's renewable sources and benefits.

Cost Control

Executive Order 13123 specifically allows the savings from energy efficiency to be used to pay for renewable energy. Agencies are encouraged to consider using some of the savings from Energy Savings Performance Contracts (ESPC) or Utility Energy Service Contracts (UESC) to buy renewable power. Buying RECs is generally the least expensive way to purchase green power, but agencies should consider making at least a small purchase through their local utility if they have a program. Agencies should submit a budget request to cover any remaining cost premium (per E.O. 13123, sec. 301).

Developing an Effective Solicitation

An agency's electricity consumption data should be part of any RFP and are required by the GSA, DESC, and Western when they help with the procurement. The purchasing agency should notify renewable power suppliers of the RFP and hold a preproposal meeting with prospective suppliers if the procurement is not standard.

Load Aggregation

Combining several facilities into one acquisition can lead to big purchases, but it is best to target these aggregation efforts only to big users. Trying to aggregate many smaller users can be difficult. It also is best to keep the procurement simple.

Supplier Relations

Utility green pricing should be seen as a partnership in which the utility and the federal purchaser work together to construct a program that meets both their needs. Investor-owned utilities are usually not able to launch their own green power programs without PUC approval. However, a large federal customer could help persuade a utility to develop a new program that would then be made available to other customers. For all electricity suppliers, federal agencies should consider requesting a customized product, in order to take advantage of large purchasing volumes.

Capturing the Benefits of the Purchase

After successfully completing a green power purchase, a federal agency usually wants to publicize its efforts. In addition to the publicity messages available to other institutions, federal agencies can spread the word that the agency is working to fulfill its part of the federal renewable energy goal. Agencies with exemplary energy management programs are eligible for FEMP awards, which enhance an agency's image both inside and outside the government.

Federal agencies are required to report annually on their progress toward meeting their energy management goals. FEMP has published guidelines for counting green power purchases and on-site renewable energy toward an agency's energy management goals (www.eere.energy.gov/ femp/ technologies/renewable_fedrequire.cfm).

Information for Potential Suppliers to the Federal Government

All federal government procurements are made competitively unless there is a compelling reason for a sole-source contract. FEMP maintains a renewable supplier list used for renewable electricity procurement notifications. Renewable energy suppliers should contact Chandra Shah, listed in the resources section of this appendix, to be added to this list. The GSA (Ken Shutika) and the DESC (John Nelson) also maintain notification lists, which are important because the GSA and DESC make most of the electricity and renewable procurements for federal sites.

Prospective suppliers are asked to provide information about their company such as completed, in progress, and planned renewable projects (type, location, size, third-party certification, etc). Suppliers also should include additional information about any projects that they believe justify a sole-source contract.

Summary of Green Power Opportunities for the Federal Government

The benefits of renewable energy are enormous, and as the nation's largest purchaser of electricity, the federal government can have a significant impact on the way that power is produced now and in the future. Federal agencies already have an unprecedented and growing range of options for purchasing renewable energy, and Executive Order 13123 directs federal agencies to increase their use of renewable energy. With more emphasis on "best value" purchasing and the explicit consideration of environmental characteristics, contracting officers now have more options than ever before to buy renewable energy. Acting in the government's—and society's—best interests, federal agencies can take advantage of the strategies outlined in this guidebook to help move the United States toward a more sustainable energy future.

Federal Resources for Green Power Information

For federal agencies buying green power, assistance is available from the following federal agencies and national labs:

DOE Regional Office FEMP representative
www.eere.energy.gov/femp/about/regionalfemp.cfm.
Green Power Network: www.eere.energy.gov/greenpower.
FEMP Web sites:
Renewable energy: www.eere.energy.gov/femp/technologies/ renewable _energy.cfm.
Renewable purchasing: www.eere.energy.gov/femp/ technologies/ renewable_purchasepower.cfm.
Design assistance: www.eere.energy.gov/femp/services/ projectassistance. cfm.
*Training:*www.eere.energy.gov/femp/technologies/renewable_training.cfm.
Financing: www.eere.energy.gov/femp/services/project_facilitation.cfm.
For assistance with program resources:
Department of Energy, Federal Energy Management Program David McAndrew, Renewable Purchasing (202) 586-7722 Anne Sprunt Crawley, Technical Assistance (202) 586-1505
For assistance issuing solicitations:
General Services Administration Ken Shutika (202) 260-9713 ken.shutika@gsa.gov
Defense Energy Support Center John Nelson (703) 767-8669 john.nelson@dla.mil
Western Area Power Administration's Federal Renewable Program
www.wapa.gov/powerm/pmrenpro.htm
Mike Cowan (720) 962-7245
cowan@wapa.gov
For technical assistance, including market intelligence, market rules, and the development of requirements and statements of work, contact
Lawrence Berkeley National Laboratory William Golove (510) 486-5229

WHGolove@lbl.gov

National Renewable Energy Laboratory Chandra Shah (303) 384-7557

chandra_shah@nrel.gov

For more information or assistance in developing a plan to enhance the security of federal facilities through the use of renewable energy, contact

John Thornton

Energy Assurance R and D Coordinator homelandsecuritycoordinator @nrel.gov (303) 384-6469

Nancy Carlisle

NREL/FEMP

nancy_Carlisle@nrel.gov 303-384-7509

Dave Menicucci

Leader, Defense Energy Support Program dfmenic@sandia.gov (505) 844-3077

In: Green Movement in Business
Editor: Karin E. Sanchez

ISBN: 978-1-60692-188-3
© 2009 Nova Science Publishers, Inc.

Chapter 2

THE GREENING OF U.S. CORPORATIONS

The Bureau of International Information Programs of the U.S. Department of State publishes a monthly electronic journal under the *eJournal USA* logo. These journals examine major issues facing the United States and the international community, as well as U.S. society, values, thought, and institutions.

One new journal is published monthly in English and is followed by versions in French, Portuguese, Russian, and Spanish. Selected editions also appear in Arabic, Chinese, and Persian. Each journal is catalogued by volume and number.

The opinions expressed in the journals do not necessarily reflect the views or policies of the U.S. government. The U.S. Department of State assumes no responsibility for the content and continued accessibility of Internet sites to which the journals link; such responsibility resides solely with the publishers of those sites. Journal articles, photographs, and illustrations may be reproduced and translated outside the United States unless they carry explicit copyright restrictions, in which case permission must be sought from the copyright holders noted in the journal.

The Bureau of International Information Programs maintains current and back issues in several electronic formats, as well as a list of upcoming journals, at http://www.america.gov/publications/ejournals.html. Comments are welcome at your local U.S. Embassy or at the editorial offices:

Editor, eJournal USA
IIP/PUBJ
U.S. Department of State 301 4th St. S.W.
Washington, DC 20547 United States of America
E-mail: eJournalUSA@state.gov

ABOUT THIS ISSUE

This issue of *eJournal USA* delves into what those familiar with the history of the environmental movement in the United States might see as a surprising trend — the way U.S. corporations in recent years have embraced environmentally friendly ways of doing business. What prompts a corporation to "go green"?

"We looked across our company and recognized that a focus on environmental technology could be a big business initiative for the company," said Jeffrey Immelt, the chief executive of General Electric, a leader in this field. "The concept we worked on at the time was this notion that green is green." So the environment has become a business opportunity, a chance to increase profits, the core of any business enterprise.

An example of the greening of U.S. corporations, Sea Gate Plaza is designed to be the first green commercial building in Fort Lauderdale, Florida.

But the story of converting corporations to green policies is more complex than that. Nongovernmental organizations (NGOs), consumers, investors, new technologies, and government policy have all played a role. NGOs and businesses are finding ways to work together to protect the environment, particularly though developing standards and green certification programs. Some corporations are responding to the desires of consumers to buy products with less impact on the environment — in their creation, packaging, marketing, use, and disposal. Many investors, too, are choosing to put their money into green businesses — sometimes for idealistic reasons; sometimes because they see that sustainable practices are actually more profitable in the long term. Recent developments in technology have made it easier to protect the environment, and many businesses have learned that a sustainable supply chain is a valuable asset. Government policies have certainly played a role, but that is not the primary focus of this journal.

Jeffrey Immelt explains the movement best when he elaborates on his company's thinking: "This is no longer a fringe topic. It's no longer a niche topic. This is now a mainstream topic that is being driven across the broad economy. Second, the technology and the service solutions are real. Some may take time to put into place, like coal gasification, sequestration, or hybrid technologies, but they are technologies that can be commercialized over the next 5 or 10 years. Finally, this interest has accelerated — sometimes driven by public policy — things like renewable performance standards. But a lot is driven by businesses that finally said, 'Let's get ahead of this theme. Let's get ahead of the trend. Let's invest before we have to because we see it coming.'"

— *The Editors*

U.S. COMPANIES EMBRACE GREEN TECHNOLOGY

Paul Nastu

For as long as companies have manufactured goods, they have looked for ways to reduce costs. corporations are beginning to realize that developments in technology are making it easier for green choices to lead to increased profits.

Paul nastu is publisher and managing editor of Environmental Leader, *an online publication that describes itself as the "executive's daily green briefing" [www. environmentalleader.com].*

Energy efficiency was about increasing profits before it was about saving the planet. Today, it takes less than half the energy to produce a dollar of economic output as it did in 1970, according to recent research from the American Council for an Energy-Efficient Economy. Over the past 20 years, steel manufacturing has seen an energy- efficiency improvement of 167 percent. The energy efficiency of computer systems has improved an incredible 2.8 million percent.

In other words, for as long as companies have manufactured goods, they have looked for ways to lower costs.

Of course, times have changed. There is new impetus for U.S. companies to make energy-efficient, or green, choices. The global scientific community has declared that global warming is very likely man-made and that the Earth's climate and ecosystems are already being affected by greenhouse gases.

What's more, public opinion seems to have turned, and people are calling for corporations to make changes. Some consumers have stated that they're even willing to pay more for corporations to produce greener products. According to Forrester Research, 12 percent of U.S. adults — some 25 million Americans — are willing to pay extra for consumer electronics that use less energy or come from a company that is environmentally friendly.

Citigroup has adopted power-saving measures that are designed to save nearly $100 million annually.

Green Building

Companies are taking green building — and the subsequent savings in energy, natural resources, and money — seriously. New technologies and the increasing importance of the U.S. Green Building Council's (USGBC) Leadership in Energy and Environmental Design (LEED) certification program, as well as new efficiency codes, are helping to drive corporate adoption.

The savings to companies can be large. Financial conglomerate Citigroup, with a real estate portfolio equaling 8.5 million square meters worldwide, has adopted such power-saving measures as turning off escalators in the lobbies of buildings and redesigning bank branches to include more natural lighting and recycled materials. The company says it can save as much as $1 per 0.09 square meter a year, or nearly $100 million annually, by making its offices use less energy.

That kind of potential savings is driving retailers such as Wal-Mart, Target, Starbucks, Best Buy, Lowe's, and REI to build prototype green-building stores. Best Buy claims that in the future, it will build only ecofriendly stores, certified by the USGBC through LEED.

Office equipment retailer Office Depot says that it has reached a 10 percent absolute reduction in carbon dioxide emissions from natural gas and electricity consumed in its North American retail stores, warehouses, and offices by installing more energy-efficient technology.

The Frito-Lay plant in Modesto, California, uses these solar panels to provide the energy to bake an estimated 145,000 bags of SunChips per day.

Green Energy

Technology advances are also leading U.S. corporations to increase the amount of alternative energy they use. And government incentives are making alternative energy, such as solar and wind power, economically feasible.

Google expects to invest hundreds of millions of dollars in renewable energy projects. The goal of the Internet search giant's RE<C (for Renewable Energy Cheaper Than Coal) initiative is to develop electricity from renewable energy sources that will be cheaper than electricity produced from coal. Google will focus initially on advanced solar thermal power, wind power, enhanced geothermal systems, and other potential breakthrough technologies.

Companies are also finding less expensive ways to incorporate green energy. Potato chip and snack-food maker Kettle Foods has installed 18 wind turbines on the roof of its new Beloit, Wisconsin, manufacturing facility. The turbines are projected to generate approximately 28,000 kilowatt-hours of power each year — enough to produce 56,000 bags of potato chips.

The nano-manufacturing technology firm Applied Materials is installing more than 1.9 megawatts of solar power generation capability on the open roof space and parking areas of its research campus in Sunnyvale, California. Once completed in 2008, Applied Materials' system will generate more than 2,330 megawatt-hours annually — enough to power 1,400 homes.

West Virginia Alloys, the largest silicon producer in the United States, has contracted with Recycled Energy Development to build an electricity-generation system that captures hot gases coming from silicon furnaces to make steam and run generators.

And at its plant in Casa Grande, Arizona, snack-food producer Frito-Lay will use methane gas to run the plant's boiler. In addition, the company will build at least 20 hectares of solar concentrators and a biomass generator.

Green Operations

To understand just how serious businesses are about reducing the amount of energy they use to run their operations, you need look no further than General Electric Company. GE has pledged to invest $1.5 billion annually on ecomagination research and development by 2010. One of four GE ecomagination commitments originally made in 2005, R and D investment has reached more than $2.5 billion since the program's inception. In May 2007, GE announced that it had doubled sales from environmentally friendly products to $12 billion over the previous two years.

Danielle Merfeld, seen here amid solar panels in Niskayuna, New York, leads GE Global Research's solar research efforts. General Electric is one of a group of corporations working under a federal program to make solar energy cost competitive by 2015.

Wal-Mart is measuring the amount of energy used to create products throughout its supply chain, including the procurement, manufacturing, and distribution process.

The retailer is initiating a pilot with a group of suppliers to look for new ways to make its entire supply chain more energy efficient.

SC Johnson, a leading cleaning products manufacturer, recently completed a transportation-logistics project that eliminated 1,882 tons of greenhouse gases over a 12-month period, used 2,098 fewer trucks, reduced fuel usage by 168,000 gallons, and saved approximately $1.6 million.

What's Ahead

Corporations are beginning to realize that green choices can mean increased profits. Some industry insiders believe that a sudden decrease in energy costs will not necessarily mean the end of the adoption of green technology, as was the case in the 1 970s when U.S. companies dabbled in green. What's more, as the United States moves closer to some form of cap and trade (a system that provides economic incentives for pollution reduction), the adoption of green technologies by corporations is bound to increase. [1]

CORPORATE EXECUTIVES ON GOING GREEN

The headquarters of Apple Inc. are located in Cupertino, California.

Rick Wagoner, GM (General Motors Corporation) Chairman and Chief Executive Officer (CEO)

"The key as we see it at GM is energy diversity — being able to offer our customers vehicles that can be powered with many different sources of energy. We must — as a business necessity — develop alternative sources of propulsion, based on alternative sources of energy, in order to meet the world's growing demand for our cars and trucks." (2007, Geneva Motor Show) *[http://www.autobloggreen.com/2007/03/06/geneva-motor-show-rick-wagoner-affirms-commitment-to-energy-div/]*

---

[1] The opinions expressed in this article do not necessarily reflect the views or policies of the U.S. government.

H. Lee Scott, Wal-Mart President and CEO

On the motivation behind the corporation's setting long-term sustainability goals: "I think two things happened. One, as we [looked] at our responsibility as one of the world's largest companies, it just became obvious that sustainability was an issue that was going to be more important than it was, let's say, last year and the years before. I had embraced this idea that the world's climate is changing and that man played a part in that, and that Wal-Mart can play a part in reducing man's impact. We recognized that Wal-Mart had such a footprint in this world, and that we had a corresponding part to play in sustainability." (2006, MSNBC interview) *[http://www. msnbc.msn.com/id/1231672 5/]*

Chad Holliday, Dupont Chairman and CEO

DuPont is committed to creating innovative materials that help builders and architects produce sustainable 'green' buildings that cost less to operate, are easier to maintain, and provide better comfort year round. At DuPont we are proud of a decade of reducing our environmental footprint. We have come a long way, certainly in reductions of waste and emissions, but also in recognizing the impact of our operations on global issues such as climate change. We define this direction as sustainable growth — the creation of shareholder and societal value while decreasing our environmental footprint along the value chains in which we operate." (DuPont Web site) *[http:// www2.dupont.com/Tyvek_construction/ en_US/products/ residential/ products/green design_resi.html]*

DuPont scientist Max Li develops new biofuels in the state-of-the-art fermentation laboratory at the DuPont Experimental Station in Wilmington, Delaware.

Steve Ballmer, Microsoft CEO

Explaining that PCs and other technology still consume far too much electricity, Ballmer said: "The lowering of energy consumption is as important for us as new uses of software and IT for the environment." (2008, CeBit Technology Show in Hannover, Germany) *[http://www. news.com/ballmer-Microsoft-is-thinking-green/2100-1 1392_3-6233152.html?tag=item]*

Steve Jobs, Apple CEO

"It is generally not Apple's policy to trumpet our plans for the future; we tend to talk about the things we have just accomplished. Unfortunately this policy has left our customers, shareholders, employees, and the industry in the dark about Apple's desires and plans to become greener. Our stakeholders deserve and expect more from us, and they're right to do so. They want us to be a leader in this area, just as we are in the other areas of our business. So today we're changing our policy." (Apple Web site) *[http://www.apple. com/hotnews/agreenerapple/]*

Jeffrey Immelt, GE (General Electric) Chairman and CEO

"We looked across our company and recognized that a focus on environmental technology could be a big business initiative for the company. The concept we worked on at the time was this notion that green is green. In other words, the time had come that, through technology, we felt like we could create a good business initiative to focus on conservation and greenhouse gas emission reduction and do good business at the same time." (2007, interview with VerdeXchange News) *[http://www. verdexchange.org/node/82]*

Alan Mulally, Ford Motor Company President and CEO

"Ford Motor Company is committed to producing a full range of fuel-efficient vehicles that emit fewer greenhouse gases, without compromising customers' choices for interior room, performance, or safety. We are focusing on sustainable technology solutions that can be used not for hundreds or thousands of cars — but for millions of cars, because that's how we can truly make a difference." (2007, Los Angeles Auto

Show) *[http://www. ford.com/about-ford/news-announcements/featured-stories/featured-stories-detail/ford-mulally-la]*

THE RISE OF CORPORATE STAKEHOLDERS
VASANTHAKUMAR N. BHAT

This General Motors HydroGen3 minivan, shown outside the state capitol building in Lansing, Michigan, has a top speed of 160 kilometers per hour. It is powered by a hydrogen fuel cell and emits only pure water.

In recent years, U.S. corporations have reduced environmental emissions and — in response to pressures from governments, investors, environmental groups, customers, and employees — are developing "cradle-to-grave" pollution prevention strategies. Increasingly, corporate leaders see that managing environmental issues effectively can be a significant source of competitive advantage and sustainable growth.

Vasa nthaku mar n. bhat is an associate professor at the Lubin School of business, pace University, new York. he is the author of The Green Corporation: The Next Competitive Advantage and Total Quality Environmental Management: An ISO 14000 Approach, as well as several articles on environmental management.

Why do American companies choose to "go green" — that is, institute a set of corporate policies that favor environmental concerns? This is a complex story that requires some understanding of how the environmental movement arose in the United States, the long debate between advocates of regulatory approaches and voluntary compliance, and the current influence of corporate stakeholders such as customers, investors, employees, environmental groups, and government officials. The bottom line is that most American corporations now believe they can create a significant source of competitive advantage and sustainable growth by having effective environmental management. Being "green," in short, is seen as good business.

These 24 solar panels provide enough electricity to completely power the house in the background, including air conditioning, heat, lights, and computers. Such sources of energy are helping pave the way for dealing with the limits of a carbon-constrained world.

The Debate over Environmental Policy

Traditionally, from the perspective of policy makers, the environment represents what economists call "a public good" — a shared benefit like national defense from which no member of society can be excluded. Because market systems do not easily produce public goods, many in the U.S. environmental movement have believed that government intervention is necessary to motivate corporations to minimize the environmental impacts of their activities. In recent years, many have also come to believe that market-based approaches, by encouraging investment and technological innovation, are likely to reap greater environmental benefits in the end. The debate over the merits of these two approaches has continued from the inception of the U.S. Environmental Protection Agency (EPA) in 1970 right to the present.

When the environmental movement started in the United States in the 1960s and 1970s, the focus was on compliance with laws and regulations. Consequently, the traditional foundation for U.S. environmental policy has been "command and control" regulations. These regulations aim to prevent environmental problems by spelling out how a company will deal with its pollution. They are implemented using enforcement, compliance, and financial incentives. Since the regulations are mandatory, command and control regimes have been very effective. They have also increased awareness among companies about the environmental impacts of their activities.

These regulations have not been without costs, however. One negative outcome has been to encourage "end-of-pipeline" solutions that reduce pollutants after they have been produced, rather than eliminate them in the first place. In addition, the regulatory approach has led to extensive litigation.

In recent years, policy makers in the United States have increasingly emphasized economic analysis to decide what type of policy instrument to choose. Flexible policy instruments allow companies to choose the most efficient alternatives to achieve policy goals. They have been used to reduce compliance costs and to achieve superior performance at a faster pace. Market-based measures such as emissions trading — a system in which government sets a total limit on a pollutant and then allows market forces to determine how individual companies will meet their share of the limit — have been introduced in the United States for emissions of sulfur dioxides and nitrous oxides, the pollution that causes acid rain. However, these measures are still based on a single media — air, water, groundwater, or land.

More than any other country, the United States uses economic analysis to fine-tune environmental policies, and it has used this analysis to require reduced emissions by several pollution sources, including power plants and diesel engines. The United States does subsidize some aspects of waste minimization, even though, in general, a polluter-pays principle — requiring industry to bear the cost of protecting the environment — is the norm.

New Strategies

From the early days of environmental concern, then, U.S. companies pursued compliance using end-of-pipe abatement-reducing pollution by cleaning up the waste produced. As cleanup became more expensive, companies started working toward pollution prevention — using materials, processes, and equipment to eliminate the production of waste.

However, pollution prevention by itself did not improve financial performance. The total quality environmental management (TQEM) approach was needed to reap the financial benefits of improved environmental performance. As part of the TQEM approach, companies implemented the environmental management system (EMS), which provides a framework to manage environmental impacts and incorporate environmental concerns into decision making throughout an organization.

More than one in five facilities have implemented EMS, according to a recent survey. In addition, 5,585 facilities have received ISO 14000 certifications that vouch for their compliance with good management practices identified by the International Organization for Standardization (ISO). And some companies are using a range of environmental tools, including environmental auditing and life-cycle analysis. By transferring their environmental expertise to their foreign affiliates and exporting environmentally beneficial technologies, companies are also reducing the global impacts of pollution.

In 2004, the United States consumed energy equivalent totaling about 17 billion barrels of oil, or 60 barrels per capita. About 86 percent of the nation's energy came from oil, coal, and natural gas. Only 14 percent came from nuclear and renewable energy. Rising oil prices and dependence on foreign sources for almost for 65 percent of crude oil have intensified the need for energy conservation and efficiency and for new sources of energy. In addition, burning fossil fuel generates carbon dioxide and other greenhouse gases. So it is imperative for U.S. companies to prepare for a carbon-constrained world.

Currently, the United States generates more than 50 percent of its electricity from coal-fired power plants and has a plentiful supply of coal. American Electric Power is pursuing innovative methods to burn coal cleanly and to sequester carbon dioxide. This will help the industry increase power production with less damage to the environment. Florida Power and Light reduced the need for 10 new power plants by increasing energy efficiency and investing in 42 wind facilities. General Motors is working on developing hydrogen-powered cars that do not produce carbon dioxide. And IBM is working on plans to conserve energy, reduce perflurocompound (PFC) emissions, use renewable energy, encourage alternate employee commuting choices, and improve the efficiency of the company's supply chain.

The Greening of U.S. Corporations

IBM Vice President Lisa Su shows a Cell microprocessor wafer. A 2007 National Medal of Technology winner, IBM is one of the corporations working to reduce its environmental footprint.

The Power of Stakeholders

The key to modern corporate motivation is a company's concern for building rapport with its stakeholders. Government policy makers, customers, environmental groups, investors, and employees constitute major stakeholders and exert pressures on shaping a firm's environmental strategy. To reach out to these groups, companies use public disclosure and consultations about their activities and their impacts on the environment.

Government: Government regulation is a major driver of environmental policy. Exponential growth in environmental laws forces companies to anticipate and make investments to meet new requirements even before the laws are passed. Most major companies have Washington lobbyists and other staff who maintain access to high-level policy making in order to reduce the likelihood of the U.S. Congress enacting harsh regulations or the environmental agencies enforcing them stringently. Studies show that the facilities that perceive environmental regulations as being stringent tend to have a higher environmental performance. In addition, such facilities are likely to opt for pollution prevention rather than endof-pipe solutions, and to invest in environmental research and development.

But since flexible programs tend to produce superior environmental results, the EPA has also introduced a number of programs such as p2 *[http://www.epa.gov/p2/]* and partnership programs *[http://www.epa.gov/p2/pubs/partnerships.htm]*. These programs encourage businesses to go beyond minimal compliance with regulations voluntarily in return for reduced costs and public recognition as environmental leaders by the EPA.

Customers: Customers, both as voters and as buyers of products and services, have a significant impact on environmental policy. According to a *USA Today/Gallup Poll* conducted in March 2007, more than 8 in 10 Americans consider that a company's environmental record should be an important factor in deciding whether to buy its products. Corporate buyers such as IBM and Baxter International, as well as government organizations, use the environmental performance of products to make their procurement decisions.

Environmental Groups: More than one in five Americans consider themselves active participants in the environmental movement. Environmental organizations are using their clout to develop tough regulations and also to extend the areas regulated. In addition to lobbying, these organizations can take other actions that encourage companies to be green.

Many of the U.S. environmental statutes incorporate a "citizen's suit" provision that allows a private citizen to sue a corporation for violating a statute or the Environmental Protection Agency for not doing its duty under environmental laws. Any citizen can go to the federal court to prevent a company from violating relevant federal laws or permit terms and to force the company's compliance with these laws. The citizen's suit has significantly increased the clout of green organizations and has attracted many more members in view of these organizations' ability to get results.

Investors: Poor environmental performance can increase costs, because companies that produce large quantities of waste tend to have a higher number of spills and hazardous waste sites, and serious compliance problems. Investors can hold corporations accountable for environmental performance by speaking directly with corporate management, filing shareholder resolutions, and voting against the management. If they are still not satisfied, they can withdraw their investment by selling their stocks.

A number of organizations have developed environmental guidelines for companies to follow. Ceres Principles *[http://www.ceres.org]*, the Equator Principles *[www.equator-principles.com]* for project financing, and the Environment and the OECD Guidelines for Multinational Enterprises *[http://www.oecd.org/dataoecd/12/1/34992954. pdf]* are examples of such guidelines.

In addition, large institutional investors such as pension funds are joining forces to consider the environmental performance of companies before they invest. For example, according to a survey by the Principles for Responsible Investment *[http://www. unpri. org]*, 88 percent of their signatories and 82 percent of asset owners consider environment-related issues before making an investment decision.

In recent years, shareholders have been successful in convincing major banks to consider the environmental risks of projects they consider financing, persuading computer manufacturers to increase the number of computers they recycle, and encouraging public utilities to invest in renewable energy.

Procter and Gamble, headquartered in Cincinnati, Ohio, defines sustainability as "ensuring a better quality of life for everyone, now and for generations to come."

Employees: Employees bear most of the impact of poor environmental practices. Attracting employees to work in unsafe surroundings is expensive, and workers and their unions often pressure companies to reduce pollution. If employees are ignored, they often respond by changing jobs or by mobilizing public support through whistle- blowing. Costs can also rise because of higher employee turnover. Companies respond by providing employee training on environmental health and safety and on environmental management systems.

Moving toward Sustainability

While there has been significant growth in the U.S. economy in recent decades, environmental performance is mixed, as reported in the Environmental Protection Agency's *2007 Report on the Environment: Highlights of National Trends*.

One area of improvement is release of toxic chemicals. According to the EPA's *2005 Toxics Release Inventory (TRI): public Data Release*, U.S. industries discharged 4.34 billion pounds of about 650 toxic chemicals in 2005. Two industries, metal mining and electric utilities, accounted for more than half of these releases. Total chemical releases in 2005 by manufacturing facilities fell by 58 percent from those of 1988, even though the number of facilities decreased by only 16 percent and the real value of shipments increased by about 13 percent. In addition, almost half of the production-related waste was either recycled or converted into energy in 2005.

Other signs of improvement: U.S manufacturers spent $14.6 billion on pollution abatement capital and operating expenditures in 1999, representing 0.4 percent of the value of shipments and about 10 percent of new capital expenditures. American companies are beginning to see green technologies as a source of profits, exporting more than $30.4 billion in environmental technologies in 2006.

For centuries, environmental degradation has gone hand-in-hand with industrialization. As a result, over time corporate policy makers have come to the realization that environmental issues are an integral part of a company's economic well-being. Many corporate executives now feel that environmental protection is essential to sustainable development and to creating a better world. Sustainability — ensuring a better quality of life for everyone, now and for generations to come, as defined by manufacturing giant Procter and Gamble — is being seen as both a business responsibility and a business opportunity in most corporate boardrooms across America.

Even though companies have focused on pollution treatment and pollution prevention in the last decades, attention has now shifted to carbon dioxide emissions and alternate energy, and this trend is likely to continue in the future. The rising price of crude oil and dependence on a significantly high percent of imported crude oil are accelerating the need for quicker solutions to these problems.

These wind turbines are located on the Oregon-Washington border and are part of the Stateline Wind Project that produces enough power to light 70,000 homes. The turbines belong to Florida Power and Light (FPL), a leading clean-energy provider that operates natural gas, wind, solar, hydroelectric, and nuclear power plants in 25 states.

NGOs AND BUSINESS — SHARED GOALS, MUTUAL TRUST
BRAD KENNEY

The National Resources Defense Council, a major environmental NGO, has praised Willard Beach in South Portland, Maine, for the city's water-quality monitoring program.

Although their friendship is relatively new, nongovernmental organizations and the business community are working together these days to forge partnerships that last. Brad Kenney is technology/environmental editor with Industry Week *magazine.*

The past two decades have brought an increase in public consciousness in the United States concerning the rising threats of global issues such as climate change and resource conservation. This same time period has also seen a flowering of the relationship between the global business community and nongovernmental organizations (NGOs), especially those whose mission is to engage the business world in order to save the planet.

What Is an NGO?

Nongovernmental organizations are loosely defined as nonprofit organizations that exist outside the control of any government, business, political party, or armed group. They can range from highly structured global organizations to loosely knit groups of local activists. Many of the best-known NGOs focus on environmental issues, while others — such as Doctors Without Borders and Amnesty International — focus on other issues of concern to the world community, such as providing medical assistance to or championing the human rights of people in need. Their funding often comes from membership dues or grants from international institutions or governments. Most observers agree that as globalization has turned the world into one interconnected network, NGOs have been effective in filling in the spaces between where government ends and business begins.

In June 2007 in Beijing, China, Coca-Cola Chief Executive Officer E. Neville Isdell announced that Coke is funding a $20-million project to conserve seven major rivers worldwide and also revamping its bottling practices to reduce pollution and water use. This project is coordinated with the World Wildlife Fund (WWF).

NGOs and the Business Community

The business world has not always been very receptive to the pressures being put on it by outside agencies, including environmentally oriented NGOs. In fact, for most of the last century, an atmosphere of distrust and mutual suspicion existed in both camps, which often stood in the way of much progress by either group. However, as global environmental issues have risen in prominence, a growing level of alarm over the increasing effects of climate change (and the potential for even more dramatic effects to come) has brought about a new era of communication and cooperation between the business and the NGO communities worldwide — and especially in the United States.

The fruits of these budding partnerships are bountiful for both sides. For instance, while the global business community presently accounts for a large environmental impact, it also has the capital resources and working efficiency to make great strides in improving operations and lessening its footprint. Unfortunately, this potential for environmental benefits can be mitigated by the very nature of the business environment. Because businesses specialize in maximizing shareholder profits in the short term, they simply may not possess the knowledge and expertise necessary to make their operations more sustainable in the long term.

NGOs, on the other hand, may not have the resources to fund large-scale improvement projects themselves. But they are staffed by subject-matter experts who can work within their organizations, as well as with the broader business community, to develop policy positions and best practices for companies and governments to follow.

Suzanne Apple, World Wildlife Fund's (WWF) vice president and managing director for business and industry, says that in recent years her organization has begun to see greater potential in working with business, rather than against it. "I think one of the things we realized is the power of the marketplace," Apple observes. "For example, if we can get the buyer community to agree to follow responsible purchasing guidelines for forestry products, we can have a greater impact than if we were out in the forests trying to stop illegal logging."

Additionally, Apple sees increased pressure from government regulations driving businesses to step up their efforts in conservation and impact reduction — issues that NGOs are in a unique position to assist them with. "With the advent of Sarbanes-Oxley and other corporate transparency regulations, businesses are looking to third parties to assist them in auditing their operations in a credible manner," Apple says.

Shared Goals

One good example of the beneficial nature of the NGO-business partnership comes from the work that the Washington, D.C.-based nonprofit Environmental Defense is doing with the world's largest retailer, Wal-Mart Inc. The shared initiative focuses on five areas: global warming, fish farming, reducing packaging waste, alternative fuel usage, and global factory operations.

Because it is necessary for human existence, water conservation is another issue that is high on the NGO agenda. In 2007, WWF signed an agreement with global beverage giant Coca-Cola Company to launch a worldwide initiative to conserve water resources and replace the water used in the production of its drinks.

And as global trade continues to grow, the NGO community is taking steps to ensure that trade is free and fair, as well as practiced sustainably, among the nations of the world. The U.S. Business Council for Sustainable Development (USBCSD — a regional arm of the World Business Council for Sustainable Development) — has in the past few years undertaken a number of outreach opportunities designed to strengthen the environmental protection aspects of global trade, particularly the growing trade between the United States and China. Whether bringing Chinese cemen t industry representatives to tour state-of-the-art U.S. factories, or working to develop a U.S.-China Sustainability Center for improving information exchange and collaboration between the two trading partners, the USBCSD has updated its focus to reflect the changing priorities of our changing times.

Shared Opportunities

By engaging in strategic partnerships such as this with heavyweights in the U.S. business community, these and other NGOs are advancing a multifaceted environmental agenda with an impact that stretches far beyond the influence they and their members could hope to have.

In return, U.S. companies that participate in and help develop these partnerships are getting invaluable assistance in implementing comprehensive environmental impact reduction programs, and they are doing so in a way that often allows them to measure and report their improvements to their suppliers, to the government, and, ultimately, to U.S. consumers — an increasing number of whom are demanding such progress from the companies whose products they purchase.

This ability to adapt to the changing needs of both business and the environment truly demonstrates the type of flexibility that only a strong partnership, built on mutual goals and shared trust, can provide.

The NGO Environmental Defense has been working with Wal-Mart, which built this experimental environmentally friendly supercenter in McKinney, Texas.

The rainwater that drains into this holding pond through pervious pavement at the Wal-Mart supercenter in McKinney, Texas, is used to nourish the landscape.

CONSUMERS DEMAND GREEN
TRACI PURDUM

The first Earth Day in New York City, April 20, 1970.

Many consumers are recognizing that their consumption affects the environment, and they are pressuring corporations to reduce the negative effects of their operations.

Traci purdum is the editor-in-chief of HVACR Business, a monthly business-management magazine geared toward heating, ventilation, air conditioning, and refrigeration contractors.

As an American business journalist, I am required by my job to be aware of consumer trends. No matter what industry I am writing for, it is the end customer that makes or breaks the free market.

Unfortunately, some consumers are fickle. The must-have widget of today will turn into tomorrow's trash — either through the natural course of fading fads or the oftentimes maddening phenomenon of instant obsolescence.

But, increasingly, consumers seem to be recognizing what their consumption does to the environment. These consumers are smart, and they want the companies with which they do business to be smart as well. That means not only creating products that help consumers organize their lives, achieve personal and business success, look their best, feel their best, and make them the envy of the neighborhood, but also that help them lower their carbon footprint.

This year marks the 38th anniversary of Earth Day, which was the brainchild of a U.S. senator who aimed to bring environmental concerns to mainstream America.

As reported on the Earth Day Network's Web site, at the time of the first Earth Day "Americans were slurping leaded gas through massive V-8 sedans. Industry belched out smoke and sludge with little fear of legal consequences or bad press. Air pollution was commonly accepted as the smell of prosperity. Environment was a word that appeared more often in spelling bees than on the evening news."

While the message was slow to make an impact back in the 1 970s, in today's world it is difficult not to be aware of — or at least curious about — the impact we are having on our limited resources. And it is that concern that has companies catering to consumers' desires to be less offensive to the environment.

This green home uses a solar electric power system with photovoltaic cells on the roof. Its environmentally conscious construction also features Lyptus wood floors made from trees that will regenerate in 20 years.

Building Green

Indeed, "green" is the new buzzword making its way into the mainstream via commercials, television shows, company dossiers, and conferences.

To be sure, at the end of 2007 I attended the U.S. Green Building Council's Greenbuild International Conference and Expo held in Chicago. The event attracted more than 20,000 environmentally conscious builders, architects, students, and media — all there to witness the sea change of the building industry.

To kick off the conference, former President Bill Clinton announced to a global audience several new partnerships to improve the energy efficiency of hundreds of millions of square meters of public and private real estate throughout the United States.

The environmental initiative has made its way to an industry infamous for depleting forests and gobbling up green spaces. Why? Because consumers demand it.

Manufacturing Green

And what consumers want, consumers get. Indeed, manufacturers are designing for the environment in order to capture consumers' dollars. General Electric Company, for example, has undertaken an ecomagination campaign to highlight the company's focus on a cleaner environment. And Nike Inc. has launched the Nike Environmental Action Team to focus on recycling, education, and innovative programs such as Reuse-A-Shoe, which recycles shoes and turns them into new products. These companies understand the power of green and what it means for their bottom lines. Being last to market with concern for resources is irresponsible at best.

But it isn't merely being environmentally friendly that matters. Companies know that the power of marketing green products is worth more to the bottom line than lowering their carbon footprints.

Touting a "greener Apple," Steve Jobs, Apple Inc.'s chief executive officer, recently penned a letter to customers noting that his company "has been criticized by some environmental organizations for not being a leader in removing toxic chemicals from its new products, and for not aggressively or properly recycling its old products. Upon investigating Apple's current practices and progress toward these goals, I was surprised to learn that in many cases, Apple is ahead of, or will soon be ahead of, most of its competitors in these areas. Whatever other improvements we need to make, it is certainly clear that we have failed to communicate the things that we are doing well."

Some pundits in the electronics industry note that the most Earth-friendly thing a company can do is increase the length of time between new hardware purchases.

In the future, consumers are going to enjoy the fruits of a battle among electronics makers who are vying for their dollars via upgrades rather than whole new — and expensive — purchases.

Traveling Green

Interestingly, consumers' concerns aren't just focused on products. How they travel and where they stay for business and holidays also may be determined by environmental impact.

Green travel and green hotel sites are popping up all over the world and are attracting more than tree-hugging globetrotters. Even casual travelers have been introduced to green initiatives in subtle ways. From the hotel room placards that urge guests to reuse bath towels and resist having housekeeping change bedsheets daily in order to conserve water, to paperless checkouts, the travel and tourism industry is cashing in on being environmentally sound. Consumers are able to feel good about their stay at a green hotel, and hotels are able to slow down their water and electric meters and enjoy smaller utility bills.

But what about air travel? Aircraft pollution in the form of ozone-depleting nitrogen and carbon dioxide has many consumers thinking twice about their mode of transportation. How do they tread lightly upon the Earth and still enjoy the convenience of airplanes?

A recent trend is carbon-offset programs. These programs are aimed at guilt-laden consumers wanting to erase their environmental sins.

For example, Continental Airlines recently launched a carbon-offsetting program, developed in partnership with nonprofit Sustainable Travel International. The voluntary program allows customers worldwide to view the carbon footprint of their booked itinerary, which Sustainable Travel International calculates from the fuel consumption of Continental's aircraft. Travelers then can make a contribution to Sustainable Travel International via one of four project portfolios:

- Gold Standard emission reduction projects managed by MyClimate, which are renewable energy and energy-efficiency

projects validated, registered, and verified following Clean Development Mechanism principles under the Kyoto Protocol
- International reforestation projects that preserve and create critical forests and that are designed using the standards set forth by the Climate, Community, and Biodiversity Alliance
- U.S. Green-e certified renewable energy projects, such as wind farms
- Or a combination of these projects.

The Green Bottom Line

What started as our ancestors' dreams to fly like birds, erect buildings that touch the sky, and pave trails across the globe grew into massive industries that in their infancy disregarded their effect on the environment — all in the name of progress. Now, like the phoenix rising from the ashes of its past lifecycle, industry is taking its cue from the environment and is attempting a rebirth — all in the name of consumer demand. .

GREEN BUILDINGS

The Chesapeake Bay Foundation's Phillip Merrill Environmental Center in Annapolis, Maryland, has won national recognition for its pioneering conservation efforts and has drawn visitors from around the world looking for ideas they can take home.

The Visionaire, shown here in an artist's rendering, is a luxury green condominium tower in New York City.

NRG Systems, a leader in wind measurement technology, included features such as solar panels and a cooling pond in its energy-efficient headquarters in Hinesburg, Vermont.

The Greening of U.S. Corporations 107

The design of PNC Bank's branch in Tarentum, Pennsylvania, uses natural light and recycled materials as part of a green building prototype the company is using to build new branch offices.

This skylight, one of many green improvements to the 1920 Brown and Jones Architects' building in Raleigh, North Carolina, tracks the sun and moves reflectors accordingly to direct light into the offices below. It is surrounded by sedum plants, which help hold rainwater on the roof for cooling.

The Las Vegas Springs Preserve is a 72-hectare national historic site with seven green buildings that meet platinum LEED (Leadership in Energy and Environmental Design) certifi cation, the best rating from the U.S. Green Building Council.

In this affordable, prefabricated small-lot home, the mkSolaire™ by Michelle Kaufmann Designs, the roofs and windows sculpt natural light and fresh air into the center of the home. The nontoxic, recyclable, and renewable materials require less energy to build and to maintain.

The David L. Lawrence Convention Center in Pittsburgh, Pennsylvania, has a sloping roof designed to pull cool air from the Allegheny River into the building and to allow hot air to rise and leave through roof vents.

The Genzyme Center, world headquarters for the biotechnology fi rm Genzyme Corporation, is one of the largest buildings to receive the platinum rating from the U.S. Green Building Council. The building's extensive use of natural light helped produce a 42 percent reduction in annual electricity costs.

These students and their teacher at Tarkington Elementary School in Chicago, Illinois, will enjoy the benefits of this living, green roof atop the school's gymnasium. Its soil and vegetation provide insulation that keeps the building warm in winter and cool in summer.

BUSINESS, INVESTORS, AND THE ENVIRONMENT
MATTHEW PATSKY AND ELIZABETH LEVY

Assistant Secretary for Energy Efficiency and Renewable Energy Andy Karsner (second from the right) joins corporate executives in the opening bell ceremonies of the New York Stock Exchange for the initial public offering of Global Alternative Energy Exchange-Traded Fund in May 2007.

Green investing, or investing with the environment in mind, is an evolving practice with a rich history. It has grown to include evaluating a company's environmental profile. Many investors use their investments to promote a green agenda.

Matthew patsky is partner and portfolio manager, and Elizabeth levy is senior environmental analyst, with Winslow Management company, a firm that specializes in green investing.

Investors play an important role in advancing the environmental activities of the companies in which they invest. Green investing, or investing with the environment in mind, is an evolving practice with a rich history. No longer just referring to avoiding companies with historical environmental liabilities, environmental investing has grown to include evaluating a company's environmental profile to aid in research on topics including projecting future growth, analyzing preparation for upcoming regulations, and assessing risk preparedness.

And many green investors are not shy about using their investments to promote a green agenda.

RISK-FOCUSED ATTENTION

During the first wave of environmental investing in the 1 980s and early 1 990s, environmental investors were concerned primarily with evaluating environmental activities from a risk perspective. The massive losses from asbestos-related claims — estimated to be more than $250 billion in the United States alone, as reported in *The Economist* in 2005 — prompted some investors to include environmental liabilities in their financial analysis, such as responsibility and provision for remediation of sites contaminated with hazardous waste that are deemed Superfund sites by the federal government. Investors began incorporating other environmental data points into their thinking, such as use and emissions of toxic and hazardous chemicals. Research organizations such as KLD and the Investor Responsibility Research Center (now part of RiskMetrics Group) provided investors with data on environmental regulatory compliance and violations, emissions of toxic chemicals, and environmental management programs.

Today, environmental investors consider not only retrospective risk from past activities and emissions, but also future environmental risks, particularly related to climate change. For many environmental investors, as well as many environmentalists, climate change has emerged as an overarching concern that encompasses others, such as fresh water use and shortage, destruction of animal habitats, and air pollution.

For the companies that investors analyze, climate change presents a series of challenges for both current business and future planning. For example, according to the weather-risk management consultancy Storm Exchange, a two-degree rise in average temperature during autumn can result in a 1 percent drop in same-store sales, a key measure that financial analysts use to judge retailers. In September 2007, the temperature was on average two degrees warmer than normal, and October 2007 had the slowest October retail sales growth in 12 years, according to the International Council of Shopping Centers.

Climate and environmental concerns are also affecting the thinking of the private equity investors that buy and sell companies. In January 2007, the Texas energy company TXU Corp. was purchased by Goldman Sachs and private equity firms Texas Pacific Group and Kohlberg Kravis Roberts. Notably, the buyers announced that they had consulted with leading environmental groups Environmental Defense and Natural Resources Defense Council, and they had agreed to cut back a controversial plan to build 11 new coal-fired power plants to a more acceptable plan for three new plants as part of the purchase agreement. With plans for new coal-fired plants having been rejected by governments in Kansas, Oklahoma, Florida, and Washington State by the end of 2007, TXU's investors' agreement seems almost prescient.

NEW OPPORTUNITIES

But instead of just looking to environmental information to help analyze risks, a new wave of environmental investors are looking at environmental protection as an opportunity, and they are investing in market sectors that barely existed even a few years ago. For example, direct investment in alternative energy-related publicly traded companies, such as through initial public offerings (IPOs) or secondary public offerings, totaled less than $1 billion globally in 2004, according to research firm New Energy Finance (NEF). In 2007, that amount soared to almost $25 billion (see chart). In 2007 alone, this flow of investment dollars directly to companies allowed the expansion of solar cell factories, the development of wind farms, the purchase of run-of-river hydroelectric projects, the planting of fuel crops, research into fuel cell commercialization, and the development of geothermal power plants, among others.

The flow of capital to these firms working to improve the environment has had a few interesting consequences for environmental investors. The first is that there are now many more companies in which environmental investors can invest. According to New Energy Finance, between 1992 and 2002, there were 30 IPOs of alternative energy-related companies raising $2 billion; in 2003-2004, 29 IPOs raised $7 billion; in 2005-2006, 92 IPOs raised $13 billion; and in 2007 alone, 61 IPOs raised $17 billion. As the universe of companies providing environmental solutions has swelled, so has the universe of investors investing in them. A variety of funds are now investing in alternative energy, including exchange-traded funds (ETFs) that invest in alternative energy indices, actively managed mutual funds, and a myriad of private equity funds, many launched in the past two years.

Even more remarkable, it is now possible for investors to make money by investing in these new technologies, which historically has not always been true. For example, the New Alternatives Fund has been focused on investing in alternative energy since 1996, longer than any of the widely tracked alternative energy indices. Between 1996 and 2004, the fund's performance was essentially flat; between 2005 and 2007, the fund's shares approximately doubled in value. Many of the indices and other funds investing in alternative energy have shown similar strong performance since 2005.

The Superfund

In 1980, 10 years after the first Earth Day, the U.S. Congress enacted the Comprehensive Environmental Response, Compensation, and Liability Act (CERCLA), which authorized the "Superfund," the federal government's program to clean up the nation's uncontrolled hazardous waste sites. It has allowed the federal government to help cities and states clean up the nation's most dangerous toxic waste sites.

To do this, the Environmental Protection Agency (EPA) works closely with communities, potentially responsible parties (polluters), scientists, researchers, contractors, and state, local, tribal, and other federal authorities. Working with these groups, EPA identifies hazardous waste sites, tests the conditions of the sites, formulates cleanup plans, and begins cleaning up identified sites.

New sites are added each year; some sites deleted from the list have been put back on the list for further cleanup. Controversies exist about its funding mechanism, its definition of "cleanup," and other issues. Still, Superfund is the first program in the world to tackle a country's 150-year industrial legacy and to make those responsible for the waste pay to clean it up.

BEFORE SUPERFUND

Love Canal is a neighborhood in Niagara Falls, New York. In the 1970s, the neighborhood had a high rate of cancer cases and birth defects. Local schoolchildren constantly were ill. The residents eventually discovered that a nearby canal was a toxic chemical dumping site. By 1978, Love Canal had drawn national media attention, and newspaper articles were calling the neighborhood "a public health time bomb."

The same year — because there was no other legal way for the federal government to help the state of New York with an environmental problem — then-President Jimmy Carter declared a federal emergency at Love Canal.

Eventually, the government relocated more than 800 families and reimbursed them for their homes. The polluter's parent corporation, Occidental Petroleum, spent more than $200 million to clean up the site, and Congress passed the law establishing Superfund in 1980.

SUPERFUND TODAY

According to Katherine Probst, senior fellow and director of Risk, Resource, and Environmental Management at Resources for the Future (an environmental policy research group in Washington, D.C.), "Most of corporate America is much more aware of the costs of not managing hazardous substances well, and Superfund liability [for polluters] has had a huge deterrent effect." Seventy percent of cleanups, she added, are paid for directly by responsible parties.

Superfund liability, Probst said, "does provide a very clear and very real incentive to manage hazardous substances properly. And that is really the purpose of a liability system, so in that sense it has been hugely effective."

— *Cheryl Pellerin is a staff writer with www.america.gov.*

The Greening of U.S. Corporations 115

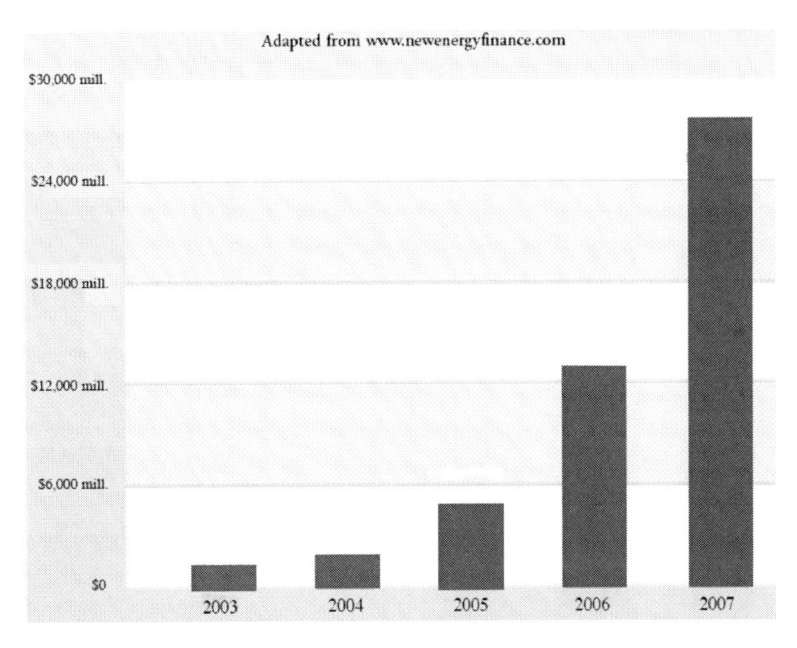

Direct Investment in Alternative Energy-Related Publicly Traded Companies.

This 1994 sign on the fence of the Love Canal dump in Niagara Falls, New York, warned visitors to keep out because of danger from hazardous waste.

In 2004, a Niagara Falls resident walks along a street near the Love Canal site, which had recently been removed from the Superfund list.

USING THEIR POWER

Many environmental investors are not shy about letting the companies in which they invest know what is on their minds. The main tool that all investors use to analyze potential investments is disclosure of information by companies. While financial information disclosure is carefully monitored by national and international regulatory bodies, disclosure of environmental information is still largely voluntary.

Groups of like-minded investors frequently join together in requests for this type of information. For example, the Carbon Disclosure Project, representing a group of investors managing $41 trillion, annually asks global corporate leaders to present their greenhouse gas emissions in a standard, comparable format. And in the United States, the Social Investment Research Analyst Network has published a statement representing firms managing $435 billion, including Winslow Management Company, calling on corporations to publish environmental and social sustainability data according to a standard set of reporting guidelines from the Global Reporting Initiative, the producer of the most widely recognized framework for sustainability reporting.

In addition to asking companies to do things, investors can also tell them to do things by filing proxy resolutions to be voted on at companies' annual meetings. Although the results of these proxy votes are nonbinding, meaning company management can ignore them, large votes can send a powerful signal to management. The Interfaith Center on Corporate Responsibility reports that as of January 2008, it had collected data on resolutions filed with more than 60 companies traded on U.S. stock exchanges for their 2008 annual meetings. The most common requests in these resolutions called for preparation of a sustainability report, reduction of greenhouse gas emissions, and the use of sustainably grown and harvested wood and paper products.

THE DEMAND FOR GREEN INVESTING

Gone are the days when environmental issues were the concerns of only students and activists. It is no longer unusual to hear the terms "emission reductions" or "pollution prevention" from investment committees or the boards of companies in which they invest.

Led by environmentally mission-oriented investors, now even mainstream investors are beginning to recognize the value of environmental information and protection. At ExxonMobil's 2007 annual meeting, for example, a shareholder-sponsored proxy resolution calling for specific greenhouse gas reduction targets garnered more than 30 percent of the votes, demonstrating the broad array of investors that are now concerned with this issue.

As the world's governments begin to negotiate a climate treaty for 2012 and beyond, the need and demand for both environmental responsibility and protection from companies will only continue to grow, and so will investor attention.

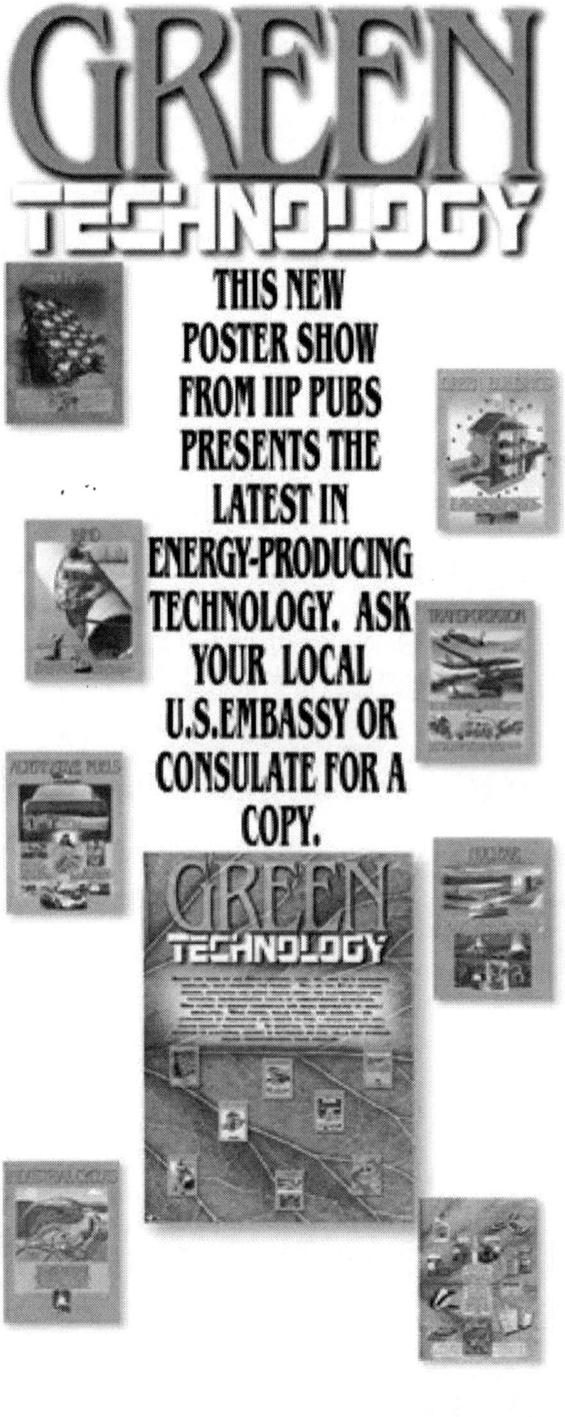

GREEN TECHNOLOGY

THIS NEW POSTER SHOW FROM IIP PUBS PRESENTS THE LATEST IN ENERGY-PRODUCING TECHNOLOGY. ASK YOUR LOCAL U.S. EMBASSY OR CONSULATE FOR A COPY.

SUSTAINABILITY WITHIN THE SUPPLY CHAIN
PATRICK C. PENFI ELD

The focus for most companies today is the development of a sustainable supply chain — one that is robust enough to support itself and actually improve the environment.

patrick c. penfield is assistant professor of supply chain practice at the Whitman School of management at Syracuse University in Syracuse, new York.

We are living in a dynamic time period and one of unprecedented growth throughout the world. Commerce between countries is increasing at exponential rates. At the same time, the world's resources are being depleted and used faster than ever before, and raw materials are becoming costlier and scarcer. Many companies are struggling with expenses while trying to increase profits.

The focus for most companies today is developing a "sustainable" supply chain — one that is robust enough to support itself and actually improve the environment.

Every company in the world has a supply chain. A supply chain is simply:

One example of a supply chain would be a car manufacturer that takes steel and other components (inputs), assembles them with labor and machines (transformation), and produces a car (output). An example of a supply chain within a service environment would be a package delivery service that takes in packages (input), stores and puts the packages en route for delivery (transformation), and then delivers the packages to the recipients (output).

The supply chain generally costs a company money, and this is why companies are so focused on sustainability. The truth is, with the increasing costs of raw material and energy, it now makes sense for companies to embrace sustainability. The return on investment is now feasible for companies so that they can employ processes that use less energy and material.

REDUCING COSTS AND ELIMINATING WASTE

Over the past year, I have been developing a model called the Sustainable Green Supply Chain. Many companies are moving in this direction, and supply chains will evolve in this area. Ideally, the goal of the supply chain model is to be environmentally friendly with the material and processes being used and to eliminate any waste within the supply chain in order to become as sustainable as possible.

By moving toward a sustainable green supply chain, companies will uncover new opportunities to reduce costs.

Another focus for many companies will be "entire" system thinking versus "component-level" thinking. Component-level thinking — a mindset that many companies are still employing — is the concept of getting the lowest price on a component and disregarding the costs to the system generated by this component. Many times, component-level thinking is employed because it's a goal or objective determined by a company or organization. If you look at the overall costs being produced by a component, however, it may become obvious that it would have made sense to spend more money up front on a more expensive component that reduces the entire system cost.

As Paul Hawken, Amory Lovins, and L. Hunter Lovins tell us in their book *natural capitalism*: "Single components are usually considered in isolation. Designing a window without the building, a light without the room, or a motor without the machine it drives works as badly as designing a pelican without the fish. Optimizing components in isolation tends to pessimize the whole system and hence the bottom line." Many companies struggle with this issue because they do not effectively measure the cost of each component within the entire system.

Some companies are employing a two-pronged approach to "green" their processes. One aspect is to move existing processes to the sustainable green supply chain model, and the other is to take new processes and design them for sustainability. The U.S. global conglomerate 3M has a program called Pollution Prevention Pays (3P). The company's policy, as described by Daniel Esty and Andrew Winston in their book *Green to Gold*, is that "anything not in a product is considered a cost. As 3M execs see it, everything coming out of a plant is either product, by-product (which can be reused or sold), or waste. Why, they ask, should there be any waste?" This is a policy that every company needs to start emulating.

ENERGY COSTS AND CONSERVATION

The major focus for many companies regarding the supply chain these days is energy. With oil trading at more than $100 per barrel, companies are having difficulties absorbing this cost. The emphasis for most companies is figuring out how to use less energy or coming up with an alternative energy option to offset the increased expense.

In the United States, ethanol, biomass, fuel cells, wind, solar, nuclear, and other various energy options are being evaluated by companies.

The other big energy initiative is conservation. Retail giant Wal-Mart has become a major sustainability player. This company has dedicated space on its Web site *[http:// walmartstores.com/]* showcasing what it is doing to help the environment. The focus has been on reducing the amount of fuel used by their trucks and stores by using alternative energy and conservation.

As stated on the Wal-Mart Web site: "We have a goal to be supplied by 100 percent renewable energy, to create zero waste, and to sell products that sustain our resources and environment." Wal-Mart is using compact fluorescent bulbs in many of its stores, employing hydrogen fuel cells for its lift trucks, placing doors on refrigeration units, replacing fluorescent lighting with LED (light-emitting diode) lighting, and conserving the power used when trucks in its fleet are idling. Wal-Mart's expectation is that the company will save millions of dollars by being sustainable.

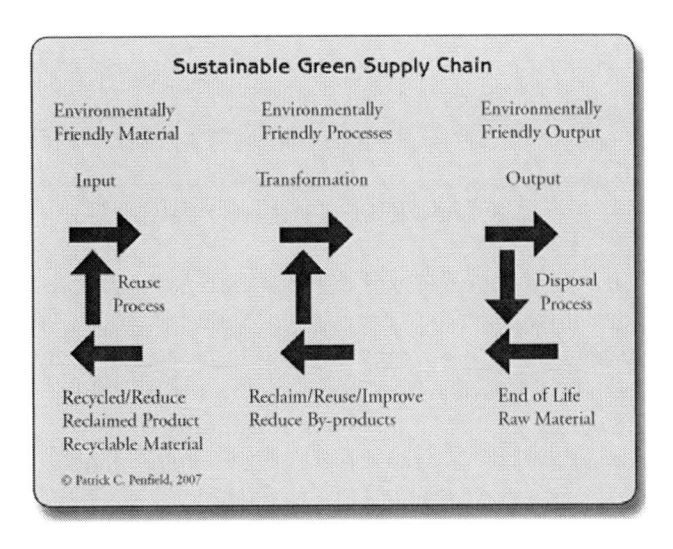

Sustainable Green Supply Chain

Input	Transformation	Output
Environmentally Friendly Material	Environmentally Friendly Processes	Environmentally Friendly Output
Reuse Process		Disposal Process
Recycled/Reduce Reclaimed Product Recyclable Material	Reclaim/Reuse/Improve Reduce By-products	End of Life Raw Material

© Patrick C. Penfield, 2007

AMD has modified a wet processing tool to use fewer chemicals and less water to clean silicon wafers.

Other companies also have focused on sustainability and reduced their costs. According to Esty and Winston, chipmaker AMD modified a "wet processing" tool to use fewer chemicals and, ironically, less water to clean silicon wafers. The process, which once used 18 gallons of water per minute, now uses fewer than six. Shoe manufacturer Timberland redesigned its shoe boxes to eliminate 15 percent of the material used in them — a dramatic savings when you ship more than 25 million pairs of shoes per year.

A Look to the Future

The big advantages for companies in becoming sustainable are reducing costs and helping the environment. In the United States, there are many pieces of environmental legislation in Congress waiting to be approved. In the meantime, companies are being proactive and focusing on sustainability. Many citizens throughout the world are demanding environmentally friendly products.

In the coming years, we can expect to see more stringent environmental standards for all companies. The future of sustainability looks green! .

POINT/COUNTERPOINT:
THE ROLE OF GOVERNMENT?

As the other articles in this issue make clear, U.S. corporations are venturing into more environmentally sustainable ways of doing business for a variety of reasons. Traditionally, however, in many countries, government regulations have been a driving force in environmental clean-up. What is the appropriate role for government in encouraging business to go green?

We asked two experts for their views on this issue. Margo Thorning is senior vice president and chief economist with the American council for capital formation in Washington, D.c. She has a ph.D. in economics from the University of Georgia, and has served with the U.S. Department of Energy, the U.S. Department of commerce, and the federal Trade commission. The council's mission is to promote economic growth through sound tax, trade, regulatory, and environmental policies.

Bob Willard is an expert on the business value of corporate sustainability strategies. The author of The Sustainability Advantage and The Next Sustainability Wave, he has a ph.D. from the University of Toronto. Willard applies business and leadership development experience from his 34-year career at IBM canada to engage the business community in avoiding the risks and capturing the opportunities associated with sustainability issues.

Much of their discussion focuses on the problem of reducing greenhouse gas emissions. We welcome comments on this topic from our readers for future publication online. please send your comments on this topic to eJournalUSA@state.gov. The limit is 200 words in English. please identify your country in signing your comment.

GOVERNMENT LEADERSHIP IN THE QUEST FOR SUSTAINABILITY
BY BOB WILLARD

The 2007 Intergovernmental Panel on Climate Change report says that we have only a few years in which to stabilize our greenhouse gases before we experience irreversible and precipitous climate change. The Millennium Ecosystem Assessment says that 60 percent of the 24 ecosystems on which we depend are being degraded or used unsustainably, and the rest are in jeopardy. According to the Global Footprint Network, humanity's ecological footprint is already 23 percent larger than what the planet can sustain, and the overshoot is growing. The United Nations Environment Program Global Environment Outlook (GEO-4) says that major persistent threats to the planet — such as climate change, the rate of extinction of species, and the challenge of feeding a growing population — remain unresolved, and all of them put humanity at risk.

These students are participating in a nationwide simultaneous tree-planting program on a 3,000-kilometer stretch of the Pan Philippine Highway. The program was sponsored by the Philippine government's Environment and Natural Resources Department.

Sustainability problems teeter on the edge of tipping points. We are in a race to see if humanity can save the world that nurtures us. Happily, solutions are known and are within our capabilities. We do not have a deficiency of solutions.

But we do have a deficiency of sustained political will. We need to stop the unsustainable practices that are precipitating this planetary emergency. We need to declare a War for Sustainability to galvanize our collective resolve. We need to bring the same level of urgency and resources to the climate, energy, and ecological crises as we have to the War on Terror. Governments need to take the lead to future-proof society.

Michael Mobbs, a consultant on eco-friendly housing developments and office projects, shown here outside his self-sufficient house in Sydney, Australia, says that government regulations are a major hurdle to encouraging more green construction.

Here are seven bold actions that address the monumental environmental and social challenges we face.

1. Integrate Education for Sustainable Development throughout the formal, non-formal, and informal education systems: Governments at all levels must implement a whole-system approach to education policies,

teacher training, facilities operations, and curriculum. The goal of the United Nations Decade of Education for Sustainable Development, 2005-2014, is to integrate the principles, values, and practices of sustainable development into all aspects of education and learning throughout the world.

Such education improves the mindsets of children and adults about the personal relevance of sustainability, the dangers of climate change and other social and environmental crises, and the urgent need for action. An informed population gives governments their mandates for change.

2. Replace the GDP with the GPI: The Genuine Progress Indicator (GPI) integrates health care, safety, a clean environment, and other indicators of well-being with the gross domestic product's (GDP) financial and economic metrics to form a more holistic assessment of national progress. Government endorsement of this annual report on the genuine wealth of a country would legitimize value other than money. Having such an assessment of the national carbon or ecological footprint would awaken people to the need for urgent action on climate change.

3. Implement ecological tax shifting: Much of our tax system is upside down: We are taxing "goods" and incenting "bads." Instead, we should tax pollution, carbon, and waste. We should incent employment, renewables, capital stock retrofits, responsible consumption, and energy efficiency. Revenue-neutral shifting of the tax burden from things we don't want to things we do want will send strong behavioral change signals.

4. Eliminate "perverse subsidies": Today, alternative energy options are discouraged by perverse subsidies to the nuclear and fossil fuel industries. Industrial countries annually subsidize the fossil fuel industry with more than $200 billion. In 2005, between $29 billion and $46 billion of that went to the U.S. fossil fuel industry alone. These are perverse subsidies because they underwrite environmentally destructive behavior. Citizens are billed twice for them — once when their taxes pay for the subsidies, and again when they bear the direct and indirect costs of environmental restoration and health care.

As with ecological tax shifting, subsidies should be shifted from the fossil fuel and nuclear industries to clean-technology industries.

5. Impose carbon caps/carbon taxes: An effective carbon-price signal could realize significant climate change mitigation potential in all sectors. Most assessments suggest that high carbon prices (20 to 50 US$/tCO2-eq), sustained or increased over decades, could lead to a power generation sector with low-GHG (greenhouse gas) emissions by 2050 and make many mitigation options in the end-use sectors economically attractive. Therefore,

governments should cap carbon emissions by company, with auctioned permits, and/or impose a carbon tax.

The Earth Atmospheric Trust proposes that governments cap global emissions, auction the pollution permits, and return dividends equally to every citizen on Earth to help reduce poverty. Another report, Option 13, also proposes a global carbon tax. Both are good ideas.

Further, governments should place a moratorium on new coal-fired plants and oils sands expansion until carbon capture and storage technologies are proven.

6. Lead by example: We need public sector leadership through government purchasing to expand demand for "green" products from "green" suppliers. Governments must lead by example by purchasing only appliances meeting rigorous energy-efficiency standards, advanced electric and hybrid vehicles with more powerful and reliable batteries, eco-friendly cleaning products, Forest Stewardship Council-certified paper with 100 percent post-consumer recycled fiber, and similar green products and services. All government buildings should be LEED (Leadership in Energy and Environmental Design) gold equivalent or higher, earning governments the right to change building codes and to demand the same standard for residential, commercial, and industrial buildings.

7. Work to alleviate poverty: Since many sustainability challenges stem from the desperate efforts by the poor in developed and developing countries who are trying to survive or improve their situation, concerted action by governments around the world to improve their living conditions could contribute to improving the environment.

A Summing up

These seven bold strokes are guided by a compell ing government vision of a better quality of life for all citizens. Rather than just preventing pollution, progress toward sustainability requires the systemic integration of environmental, social, and economic considerations in decision making at all levels in society.

Governments need to deploy a much more comprehensive set of policies to bolster efficiencies and productivity, reduce resource use, prevent pollution, and mobilize citizens. Governments have an important leadership role to ensure that market forces send signals that encourage sustainable corporate, institutional, and individual behavior, and punish the opposites.

The U.S. Environmental Protection Agency (EPA) encourages green building by its certification of energy-efficient construction. This house in Monroe, Michigan, is an EPA-certified five-star energy home.

GREENING BUSINESS INVESTMENT:
HOW ABOUT A CARROT?
BY MARGO THORNING

Reducing the growth of U.S. greenhouse gas emissions, a central environmental issue, while promoting economic growth are important goals for policy makers all over the world. The U.S. business sector is, for the most part, on board with the idea that companies should do their share to slow the growth of U.S. greenhouse gas emissions (GHGs). In 2002, the Bush administration committed the United States to reducing GHG intensity (the amount of energy needed to produce a dollar of GDP) by 18 percent between 2002 and 2012, and the United States is on track to exceed that target.

Accelerating the rate of GHG reduction will, none the less, require stronger efforts by industry, electric utilities, households, and government. Implementing a strategy which reduces the cost of capital for clean energy investments, for research and development (R and D), and for demand side management could pay high dividends in terms of stronger U.S. economic growth and reduced energy intensity — without slowing economic growth and increasing unemployment.

Impact of Mandatory Programs for GHG Reduction

Many current legislative proposals rely on a "cap and trade" approach to reducing emissions, while a few proposals call for a tax on carbon emissions. These proposals, if enacted, are likely to slow the growth of GDP and employment in the United States. As noted in a 2007 Congressional Budget Office report, *Issues in Climate Change*: "Obtaining allowances — or taking steps to cut emissions to avoid the need for such allowances — would become a cost of doing business for firms that were subject to the CO2 cap. However, those firms would not ultimately bear most of the costs of the allowances. Instead, they would pass along most such costs to their customers (and their customers' customers) in the form of higher prices."

Many pundits think the U.S. economy is near (or possibly already in) a recession. As policy makers attempt to rally the U.S. economy during this difficult period, it may be wise to consider some "carrots" to help companies make the kind of green investments in plant and equipment and R and D that will not only reduce the growth in GHGs but also raise productivity and economic growth.

The Role of Economic Growth and Technology in GHG Reduction

Many policymakers overlook the positive impact that economic growth can have on GHG emission reductions. For example, in 2006, while the U.S. economy grew at 3.3 percent, CO2 emissions fell by 1.3 percent Overall, energy use only declined by 0.9 percent, indicating the U.S. economy is becoming less carbon intensive even without mandatory emission caps.

Technology development and deployment offer the most efficient way to reduce GHG emissions and a strong economy tends to pull through capital investment faster. There are only two ways to reduce CO2 emissions from fossil fuel use: use less fossil fuel or develop technologies to use energy more efficiently to capture emissions or to substitute for fossil energy. There is an abundance of economic literature demonstrating the relationship between energy use and economic growth, as well as the negative impacts of curtailing energy use. Over the long-term, new technologies offer the most promise for affecting GHG emission rates and atmospheric concentration levels. Providing better tax treatment for R and D in the United States would be a positive step, for example, making the R and D tax credit permanent would encourage sustained longer term programs which could lead to technological breakthroughs.

The Role of International Partnerships

Research by David Montgomery and Sugandha Tuladhar of CRA International makes the case that agreements such as the Asia-Pacific Partnership on Clean Development and Climate (AP6), an agreement signed in 2005 by India, China, South Korea, Japan, Australia, and the United States, offers an approach to climate change policy that can reconcile the objectives of economic growth and environmental improvement for developing countries. Together, the AP6 partners have 45 percent of the world's population and emit 50 percent of man-made CO_2 emissions. The projections of very strong growth in greenhouse gases in developing countries over the next 20 years mean that there is enormous potential for reducing emissions through market-based mechanisms for technology transfer.

Montgomery and Tuladhar note that there are several critical factors for ensuring the success of an international agreement which relies strongly on private-sector investment for success. Their research shows that institutional reform is a critical issue for the AP6, because the lack of a market-oriented investment climate is a principal obstacle to reducing greenhouse gas emissions in China, India, and other Asian economies. China and India have both started the process of creating market-based economic systems, with clear benefits in the form of increased rates of economic growth. But the reform process has been slow and halting, leaving in place substantial institutional barriers to technological change, productivity growth, and improvements in emissions. The World Bank and other institutions have carried out extensive investigations about the role of specific institutions in creating a positive investment climate. These include minimizing corruption and regulatory burdens, establishing an effective rule of law, recognition of intellectual property rights, reducing the role of government in the economy, removing energy price distortions, and providing an adequate infrastructure and an educated and motivated labor force.

The Importance of Technology Transfer for Emission Reductions

As described above, technology is critically important because emissions per dollar of income are far larger in developing countries than in the United States or other industrial countries. This is both a challenge and an opportunity. It is a challenge because it is the high emissions intensity — and relatively slow or non-existent improvement in emissions intensity — that is behind the high rate of growth in developing country emissions.

Opportunities exist because the technology of energy use in developing countries embodies far higher emissions per dollar of output than does technology used in the United States; this is true of new investment in countries like China and India as well as their installed base. The technology embodied in the installed base of capital equipment in China, for example, produces emissions at about four times the rate of technology in use in the United States. China's emissions intensity is improving rapidly, but even so its new investment embodies technology with twice the emissions intensity of new investment in the United States.

Strategies for Promoting Institutional Change

Although it is clear that there is a relationship between institutions, economic growth, and greenhouse gas emissions, there is no general formula that can be applied to identify the specific institutional failures responsible for high emissions per unit of output in a specific country. If there is to be progress on institutional reform, at a minimum the key actors or stakeholders — concerned businesses; other groups with influence on opinion and policy in China, India, and other developing countries (including local and regional governments); and national governments — must agree on the nature and scope of the problems and on reforms required to address the problems and identify concrete actions that each government will take to bring about institutional reforms.

For example, making progress on implementing the AP6 can be accelerated if the governments of Australia, Japan, and the United States would fund research on topics such as the investment climate; the level of technology embodied in new investment; the role of foreign direct investment and potential energy savings from technology transfer; and the nature and impacts of pricing distortions on energy supply, demand, and greenhouse gas emissions in China and India. Government support for research to make clear the direct consequences of proposed reforms for energy efficiency and the benefits of a market based investment climate for the overall process of economic growth would also be helpful.

Broadening the International Partnership to Include All Major Emitters

At the G-8 Summit in Germany last year, policy makers agreed to take a series of steps toward GHG reductions. Recognizing that 85 percent of all emissions come from about 15 countries, G-8 leaders agreed to convene the major energy-consuming countries to agree on a new international framework by the end of 2008. The leaders agreed to work toward a long-term global goal for reducing GHGs and to accelerate the development and deployment of clean energy

technologies. They also agreed to work towards the reduction and/or elimination of tariff and non-tariff barriers to environmental goods and services through the WTO Doha negotiations. Other points of agreement included developing and implementing national energy efficiency programs and advancing international energy efficiency cooperation as well as pursuing joint efforts in key sectors such as sustainable forestry, power generation, transportation, industry, and buildings. Finally, they agreed to enhance cooperation with developing countries to adapt to climate change.

IN CONCLUSION

To be effective, policies to reduce global GHG emission growth must include both developed and developing countries. Polices which enhance technology development and transfer are likely to be more widely accepted than those that require sharp, near-term reductions in per capita energy use. Extending the framework of the Asia-Pacific Partnership on Clean Development and Climate to other major emitters will allow developed countries to focus their efforts where they will get the largest return, in terms of emission reductions for the least cost.

Finally, if the United States does adopt a mandatory greenhouse gas emissions reduction program, serious consideration should be given to implementing a carbon tax rather than an EU-style cap and trade system. A key component of any mandatory U.S. program should be allowing emissions to increase as both economic growth and U.S. population increase.

BIBLIOGRAPHY

Additional Readings on Green Corporations

DesJardins, Joseph R. *business, Ethics, and the Environment: Imagining a Sustainable future*. Upper Saddle River, NJ: Pearson Prentice Hall, 2006.

Dumaine, Brian. *The plot to Save the planet: how Serious money, Visionary Entrepreneurs, and corporate Titans Are creating real Solutions*. New York: Crown Business, 2008.

Ellin, Abby. "M.B.A.'s With Three Bottom Lines: People, Planet, and Profit." *The new York Times* (8 January 2006): p. A22.

Engardo, Pete. "Beyond the Green Corporations." *business Week*, issue 4019 (29 January 2007): pp. 50-64.

Epstein, Marc J. *making Sustainability Work: best practices in managing and measuring corporate Social, Environmental, and Economic Impacts*. Sheffield, UK: Greenleaf Publishing; San Francisco, CA: Berrett-Koehler Publishers, 2008.

Esty, Daniel, and Andrew Winston. *Green to Gold: how Smart companies Use Environmental Strategy to Innovate, create Value, and build competitive Advantage*. New Haven, CT: Yale University Press, 2006.

Gibson, Kevin, ed. *business Ethics: people, profits, and the planet*. Boston: McGraw-Hill, 2005.

Gunther, Marc. "Green Is Good: The Companies." *fortune*, vol. 155, no. 6 (2 April 2007): pp. 42-72

Harvard Business Review on Green Business Strategy. Boston: Harvard Business School Press, 2007.

Pernick, Ron, and Clint Wilder. *The clean Tech revolution*. New York: HarperCollins, 2007.

Prahalad, C.K. *The fortune at the bottom of the pyramid*. Upper Saddle River, NJ: Wharton School Publishing, 2006.

Savitz, Andrew W., and Karl Weber. *The Triple bottom line: how Today's best-run companies Are Achieving Economic, Social, and Environmental Success — and how You can Too*. San Francisco, CA: Jossey-Bass, 2006.

Internet Resources

Online Sources for Information About Green Corporations

American Council for an Energy-Efficient Economy A nonprofit organization dedicated to advancing energy efficiency as a means of promoting economic prosperity and environmental protection. *http://www.aceee.org/*

Clean Edge
Helps companies, investors, and governments understand and profit from clean technologies. *http://www.cleanedge.com/*

CFO.com — Corporations and the Environment
A special issue of the online journal *cfo.com* with articles on sustainability and green buildings. *http://www.cfo.com/guides/ guide.cfm/ 3214842?f=insidecfo*

Eco-Patent Commons
An initiative of the World Business Council for Sustainable Development to create a collection of patents on technology that protects the environment. *http://www.wbcsd.org/templates/TemplateWbcSD5/layout.as p?type=p and menuId=mTQ3nQ and doopen= 1 and clickmenu=1 eftmenu*

GreenBiz.com
An information clearinghouse on sustainable business practices.
http://www.greenbiz.com/

GreenBiz.com — State of Green Business 2008
A report on the quest of corporations and businesses to become greener and more environmentally responsible. The GreenBiz Index, a set of 20 indicators of progress, tracks the resource use, emissions, and business practices of U.S. companies.
http://www.stateofgreenbusiness.com/

GreenBiz Leaders
Provides examples of how companies of all sizes and sectors align environmental responsibility with business success.
http://www.greenbizleaders.com/

Green Energy
News stories from the *San Jose mercury news* about companies that are exploring new green technologies. *http://www.mercurynews.com/ greenenergy*

Green Power Partnership
A program of the U.S. Environmental Protection Agency that provides information to companies about consuming energy from green sources to help

reduce the environmental impacts of electricity use and support the development of renewable-generation capacity. *http://www.epa.gov/greenpower/toplists/fortune500.htm*

MSNBC — Going Green
A collection of online articles about green technologies and their use.
http://www.msnbc.msn.com/id/17950339/

The Source for Renewable Energy
An online buyer's guide and business directory to more than 12,000 renewable energy businesses and organizations worldwide.
http://energy.sourceguides.com/index.shtml.

U.S. Business Council for Sustainable Development A nonprofit association of businesses whose purpose is to deliver collaborative projects that help its members and partners demonstrate leadership in the United States on sustainable development and realize business value. *http://www.usbcsd.org/*

U.S. Green Building Council
A nonprofit corporation dedicated to sustainable building design and construction.
http://www.usgbc.org/

World Business Council for Sustainable Development A CEO-led global association of some 200 companies dealing with business and sustainable development. *http://www.wbcsd.org/*

Online Reading

Borden, Mark, Jeff Chu, Charles Fishman, Michael A Prospero, and Danielle Sacks. "50 Ways To Green Your Business." *fast company* (November 2007). Discusses options for cleaning up business. *http://www.fastcompany.com/magazine/120/50-ways-togreen-your-business.html*

Coal-Based Generation Stakeholders Group. "A Vision for Achieving Ultra-Low Emissions From Coal-Fueled Electric Generation" (January 2005).
The coal industry and its customers: how they plan to meet America's energy and environmental needs by cleaning up their acts.
www.nma.org/pdf/coal_vision.pdf

Hymowitz, Carol, moderator. "Corporate Social Concerns: Are They Good Citizenship, Or a Rip-Off for Investors?" *The Wall Street Journal online* (6 December 2005).
Dialogue about corporations' environmental responsibility — includes Benjamin Heineman Jr., then senior vice president of General Electric; Ilyse Hogue,

director of the Rainforest Action Network's Global Finance Campaign; and Fred Smith Jr., president and founder of the Competitive Enterprise Institute. http://online.wsj.com/public/article/ SB113355105439712626.html?mod=todaysjree_feature

"The McKinsey Global Survey of Business Executives: Business and Society." *The mcKinsey Quarterly* (January 2006).

Report on a poll that found overwhelming acceptance by businesses of responsibility for more than making profits. www.mckinseyquarterly.com/article_page.aspx?l2=39 and l3=2 9 and ar=1741 and pagenum= 1

National Public Radio — How Environmentalists Shaped TXU Deal

An interview with Fred Krupp, president of

Environmental Defense, about winning environmental commitments from suitors of a Texas electric utility. http://www.npr.org/templates/story/story.php?storyId=7615616

Social Investment Forum. "2005 Report on Socially Responsible Investing Trends in the United States" (24 January 2006).

A biennial report that surveys investors who care about more than the bottom line.

www.socialinvest.org/pdf/research/Trends/2005%20 Trends%20report.pdf

U.S. Climate Action Partnership — A Call for Action Recommendations from the U.S. Climate Action Partnership, a coalition of major corporations and environmental groups working for national legislation in the United States to slow, stop, and reverse the growth of greenhouse gas.

http://www.us-cap.org/climatereport.pdf

Filmography

Green: The New Red, White and Blue http://www.imdb.com/title/tt1024204/
Director: David Hickman
Running time: 90 minutes
Synopsis: new York Times columnist Thomas L. Friedman looks at various "green" technologies being adopted
by American businesses to reduce the output of the greenhouse gas carbon dioxide and ultimately to reduce global warming and ensure political stability throughout the world.

Green Is the Color of Money http://www.imdb.com/title/tt1054598/
Director: Ben Shedd
Running time: 33 minutes
Synopsis: Widescreen documentary about designing and building one of the world's most energy-efficient, high- performance buildings, the Banner

Bank Building in Boise, Idaho. Built for standard costs using standard parts put together in an integrated way, this 11-story building shows that building green is good business and good for the environment.

In: Green Movement in Business
Editor: Karin E. Sanchez

ISBN: 978-1-60692-188-3
© 2009 Nova Science Publishers, Inc.

Chapter 3

EPA'S GREEN POWER PARTNERSHIP

An Environmental Choice for Your Organization

Addressing climate risk is increasingly recognized as an important strategic issue for businesses and other organizations. Green power purchasing can reduce your organization's climate risk and identify your organization as an environmental leader to important stakeholder groups, such as customers, Wall Street analysts, shareholders, investors, government officials, and employees. The U.S. Environmental Protection Agency's (EPA's) Green Power Partnership is ready to assist you in determining if a green power purchase is right for your organization.

REDUCING THE RISK OF CLIMATE CHANGE

EPA's Green Power Partnership is a voluntary program helping to increase the use of green power among leading U.S. organizations. Organizations are encouraged to purchase green power as a way to reduce the environmental impacts associated with conventional electricity use.

The Green Power Partnership works with hundreds of leading organizations, including Fortune 500 companies, local, state, and federal government agencies, manufacturers and retailers, trade associations, as well as a growing number of colleges and universities. Partners are purchasing billions of kilowatt-hours (KWh) of green power annually, which has the equivalent impact of removing the emissions of hundreds of thousands of passenger cars from the road each year.

Your organization can benefit from partnering with EPA's Green Power Partnership by taking advantage of the credibility, expert advice, recognition, and up-to-date market information that EPA provides.

WHAT IS GREEN POWER?

Clean Renewable Energy Green power is electricity generated from environmentally preferable renewable resources, such as solar, wind, geothermal, low-impact biomass, and low-impact hydro resources. **An Environmental Choice** Conventional electricity use can be one of the most significant environmental impacts associated with your organization's operations. A green power purchase is one of the easiest ways for an organization to reduce its carbon footprint. **Supporting Domestic Energy Supply** A green power purchase helps to accelerate the development of new, domestic renewable energy sources, while playing an important role in the security of America's energy supply.

WHY ARE ORGANIZATIONS BUYING GREEN POWER?

Differentiation and Competitiveness

Whole Foods Market, a leading grocery store chain, strives to "satisfy and delight" its customers through inviting store environments, wise environmental practices, and retail innovation. In part, Whole Foods is accomplishing this by implementing a store-level green power purchasing strategy that allows store managers to respond to local customer needs, stay competitive, and differentiate their retail environment from competitors.

Climate Change Commitment and Energy Stability

As part of its broader environmental strategy, Johnson and Johnson, a leading healthcare products manufacturer, has committed to reduce its carbon dioxide emissions 7 percent below 1990 levels by 2010. Johnson and Johnson believes that investing in green power is an excellent strategy to help the company achieve its corporate environmental leadership goals, as well as a good business decision because it provides the company with a reliable supply of energy that exhibits long-term price stability.

A Cost-Effective Energy Strategy

The U.S. Air Force's green power purchase of over 300,000 MWh annually is playing an important part in controlling its long-term energy costs. For example, Edwards Air Force Base in California purchases 138,000 MWh annually, enough to cover 60 percent of its power needs. The Base is utilizing long-term fixed-price green power contracts as a financial hedge against electricity market volatility and estimates its dollar savings over a five-year purchase period at almost $42 million.

Local Impact and Community Leadership

The University of Pennsylvania understands the important role it plays within the local community and sees green power as an opportunity to demonstrate its environmental leadership. By purchasing green power, the University of Pennsylvania is able to effectively engage local stakeholders, protect the environment, and take a leadership position in supporting a sustainable future. In the same way, other organizations are also recognizing that green power purchasing is one of the easiest and most cost-effective options to make a measurable impact within their local communities.

BENEFITS FOR GREEN POWER PARTNERS

EPA's Green Power Partnership is ready to assist you in achieving your environmental goals through a green power purchase. The Green Power Partnership offers the following assistance to organizations that join the Partnership.

Expert Advice

EPA's Green Power Partnership will assist you in identifying the green power products that best meet your organization's goals. EPA is committed to making your green power purchase as easy as possible by:

- Saving you time, effort, and cost by identifying green power products that meet your organization's goals
- Providing relevant and timely answers to your questions

Publicity and Recognition

The Green Power Partnership actively promotes and recognizes Green Power Partners as environmental leaders. Your organization can benefit from EPA's recognition and publicity efforts by:

- Identifying your organization as an environmental leader
- Capturing positive attention in communities where you operate
- Differentiating your organization and its brand from the competition
- Increasing your organization's competitiveness through sustainable management practices

Tools and Resources

EPA offers organizations a variety of tools and information located on the Partnership website (www.epa.gov/ greenpower). EPA's tools and resources can be invaluable by:

- Explaining and taking the guesswork out of your green power purchase
- Assisting you in promoting the concept of green power internally and externally
- Providing you with a means to estimate the environmental benefits of switching to green power

Credibility

Participation in the Green Power Partnership signifies that your organization's green power purchase meets nationally accepted standards in terms of size, content, and resource base. Partnering with EPA's Green Power Partnership can provide great value to your organization by:

- Allowing you to compare your green power commitment to others
- Increasing stakeholders' confidence in your green power purchase

Why Buy Green Power?

Purchasing green power is an easy and effective way for your organization to reduce the environmental impact of its operations.

- Long-term green power contracts can provide a hedge against electricity price volatility and help ensure energy price stability.
- Green power is an effective way to differentiate your organization and its brand from competitors.
- A green power purchase can generate goodwill, pride, and loyalty among employees, customers, and communities.
- A green power purchase can earn your organization significant public relations benefits, including favorable coverage in local and national media.

Why Buy Green Power?

EPA's Green Power Partnership is ready to assist you in achieving your environmental goals through a green power purchase. The Green Power Partnership offers the following assistance to organizations that join the Partnership.

Join the Green Power Partnership

EPA invites your organization to join the hundreds of other U.S. organizations that are improving their environmental performance and reducing the risks associated with climate change by switching to green power.

It is easy for organizations to join EPA's Green Power Partnership:

- A green power purchase involves little to no complicated logistics
- Minimal staff time is required to initiate or maintain a green power purchase
- Joining the Partnership entails completing a simple voluntary Partnership agreement—no contract

Join other leading U.S. organizations and partner with EPA today! After signing a partnership agreement, Partners have one year to purchase green power at a level that meets or exceeds Partnership benchmarks, measured as a percentage of total annual electricity consumption (as outlined in the chart below).

Earned Recognition

The Green Power Partnership promotes the actions of its Partners through a variety of earned recognition opportunities.

- The Top 25 Partner List recognizes those Partners who have completed the largest green power purchases nationally within the Partnership. Due to its wide distribution, the list provides Partners with measurable recognition.
- The Top 10 Sector Lists acknowledge the leadership of Partners within various sectors. An organization holding a position on a Top 10 Sector List demonstrates to stakeholders— employees, customers, and investors —that their organization is an environmental leader.
- The Green Power Leadership Awards are competitive awards that recognize outstanding commitments and achievements in the green power marketplace. EPA and the U.S. Department of Energy (DOE) sponsor these awards annually and recognize market participants in the following categories: Green Power Purchaser, Green Power Partner of the Year, Green Power Supplier, and Green Power Market Development Awards.

Green Power Purchase Requirements

Your Organization's Baseload If your annual electricity use in kilowatt-hours is...	Green Power Partner Requirements You must, at a minimum, purchase this much green power within one year of joining the Partnership	Green Power Leadership Club Requirements You must, at a minimum, purchase this much green power
≥100,000,001 kWh	2% of your use	20% of your use
10,000,001 - 100,000,000 kWh	3% of your use	30% of your use
1,000,001 - 10,000,000 kWh	6% of your use	60% of your use
≤1,000,000 kWh	10% of your use	Not Applicable

In addition, the minimum Partner and Leadership Club purchase requirements must be entirely met with power from "new" renewable facilities (i.e., installed after 1/1/1997).

INDEX

A

abatement, 89, 94
access, 16, 46, 68, 91
accessibility, 77
accounting, 15, 43
accounting standards, 43
acid, 89
acquisitions, 68
administration, 68
adults, 80, 126
advertising, 8, 14, 47
affiliates, 44, 45, 90
aggregation, 68, 72
agricultural, 17, 61
agricultural crop, 61
agriculture, 18, 57
aid, 112
air, vii, 2, 5, 18, 37, 40, 47, 48, 54, 88, 89, 101, 104, 108, 109, 113
air emissions, vii, 3, 40, 47
air pollutant, 5
air pollutants, 5
air pollution, vii, 3, 18, 113
air quality, 7
air travel, 104
Aircraft, 104
Airlines, 104

alternative, ix, 2, 16, 25, 54, 70, 82, 84, 99, 114, 121, 126
alternative energy, 54, 82, 114, 121, 126
alternatives, 24, 89
analysts, 113, 139
animal waste, 61
appendix, x, 2, 31, 59, 61, 73
application, 11
appropriations, 70
Arizona, 82
asbestos, 112
Asia, 130, 132
Asian, 130
assessment, 34, 69, 126
assets, 54
assumptions, 70
atmosphere, 55, 56, 57, 98
auditing, 12, 98
Australia, 125, 130, 131
authority, 59, 60, 63
automobiles, 5
availability, 12, 13, 23, 40, 63
awareness, 89

B

banks, 93
barriers, ix, 2, 38, 40, 130, 132
batteries, 127

battery, 7
behavior, 126, 127
behavioral change, 126
Beijing, 97
bell, 111
benchmarks, 12, 45, 144
benefits, viii, ix, 1, 2, 3, 4, 9, 14, 15, 22, 25, 26, 27, 28, 29, 30, 31, 34, 37, 38, 39, 41, 42, 43, 44, 46, 47, 49, 62, 63, 71, 73, 89, 90, 98, 130, 131, 142, 143
benign, vii, 3
biofuels, 61, 85
biomass, vii, 3, 5, 13, 17, 18, 23, 26, 35, 37, 52, 59, 61, 71, 82, 121, 140
biotechnology, 109
birds, 105
blackouts, 7
BLM, 71
blocks, 13
Boston, 133
budding, 98
buildings, 17, 21, 24, 53, 70, 81, 85, 105, 108, 109, 127, 132, 134, 136
bulbs, 121
bundling, 35
Bureau of Land Management, 71
Bureau of Land Management (BLM), 71
burn, 90
burning, 26, 55, 57, 90
Bush administration, 128
business environment, 98
buyer, 15, 43, 98, 135

C

campaigns, 44, 47
Canada, 53
capacity, viii, 4, 11, 14, 26, 35, 58, 135
capital cost, 18, 51
capital expenditure, 42, 94
capitalism, 120
caps, 126, 129
carbon, viii, 3, 15, 33, 42, 43, 55, 57, 81, 88, 90, 95, 102, 103, 104, 117, 126, 127, 129, 132, 136, 140

carbon dioxide, viii, 3, 42, 43, 55, 57, 81, 90, 95, 104, 136, 140
carbon emissions, 33, 127, 129
case study, 18
cash flow, 53
casting, 32
Catholic, 22
cation, 108
CEC, 53
cell, 36, 87, 114
centralized, 10
CEO, 20, 84, 85, 86, 135
certificate, 33, 34, 49, 58
certification, 4, 6, 8, 14, 16, 20, 26, 27, 32, 33, 40, 47, 58, 65, 73, 78, 80, 128
certifications, 90
Chad, 85
channels, 44, 45
chemicals, 94, 103, 112, 122
children, 126
China, 97, 99, 130, 131
CHP, 18, 55
Cincinnati, 93
citizens, 63, 122, 127
civic leadership, 8
civilian, 68
Clean Air Act, 49
Clean Development Mechanism, 105
clean energy, 128, 132
clean-energy, 95
cleaning, 83, 89, 127, 135
cleanup, 89
climate change, 43, 56, 85, 96, 98, 112, 113, 123, 126, 130, 132, 143
CO2, 129, 130
coal, vii, 3, 56, 79, 82, 90, 113, 127, 135
coastal areas, 57
Coca-Cola, 97, 99
codes, 80, 127
Coke, 97
collaboration, 99
collateral, 46
colleges, 139
combustion, 5, 17, 18, 35, 55
commerce, 123

Index

commercial rate, 39
commercialization, 114
commercials, 103
commodity, 15, 30
communication, 98
communities, 98, 141, 142, 143
community, 4, 8, 17, 55, 77, 79, 96, 97, 98, 99, 123, 141
competition, 23, 30, 55, 57, 66, 142
competitive advantage, 87, 88
competitive markets, 12, 13, 25
competitiveness, 142
compliance, 34, 47, 62, 88, 89, 90, 92, 112
components, 45, 119, 120
composition, 25
computer systems, 79
concentration, 10, 57, 129
concrete, 131
conditioning, 88, 101
confidence, 47, 143
conflict, 7
Congress, iv, 91, 122
Congressional Budget Office, 129
consciousness, 96
consensus, 6
conservation, 9, 22, 25, 30, 53, 86, 90, 96, 98, 99, 105, 121
constraints, 15, 16, 24, 35
construction, 16, 39, 41, 85, 102, 125, 128, 135
consultants, 21, 36
consumer electronics, 80
consumer protection, 47
consumers, vii, 3, 6, 47, 48, 55, 78, 80, 99, 101, 102, 103, 104
consumption, 21, 22, 54, 58, 59, 72, 86, 101, 104, 126, 144
contractors, 34, 45, 67, 101
contracts, 23, 38, 41, 67, 68, 141, 143
control, 37, 66, 89, 97
conversion, 17
cooking, 5
cooling, 106, 107
corporations, 78, 79, 80, 82, 83, 84, 87, 88, 91, 92, 101, 117, 123, 134, 135, 136

corruption, 130
cost of power, 29
cost saving, 71
cost-benefit analysis, 53
cost-effective, 34, 36, 37, 53, 70, 141
costs, ix, 1, 7, 8, 10, 11, 12, 16, 17, 18, 22, 26, 28, 30, 37, 38, 39, 42, 60, 64, 70, 79, 83, 89, 92, 109, 119, 120, 122, 126, 129, 137, 141
coverage, 53, 143
covering, 70
credibility, 12, 27, 45, 140
credit, 33, 36, 38
criticism, 12, 14
crops, 61, 114
crude oil, 90, 95
curriculum, 126
customers, vii, 3, 8, 28, 30, 36, 40, 44, 45, 46, 56, 57, 58, 62, 63, 67, 68, 69, 71, 72, 84, 86, 87, 88, 91, 103, 104, 129, 135, 139, 140, 143, 144

D

danger, 115
database, 47
debt, 53
debt service, 53
decision makers, ix, 2, 20, 71
decision making, 90, 127
decisions, 28, 47, 71, 92
defense, 88
deficiency, 124
definition, 5, 32, 61
degradation, 94
delivery, 15, 119
demand, viii, 4, 10, 21, 26, 30, 36, 47, 58, 63, 84, 103, 105, 117, 127, 128, 131
Department of Defense, 68
Department of Energy, ix, 2, 15, 23, 43, 46, 50, 53, 54, 61, 74, 123, 144
Department of Energy (DOE), 144
Department of State, 77
depreciation, 42
deregulation, vii, 3, 68

destruction, 113
developed countries, 132
developing countries, 127, 130, 131, 132
diesel, 7, 89
diesel engines, 7, 89
direct investment, 114
direct mail, 44
disclosure, 91, 116
displacement, 26
distortions, 130, 131
distributed generation, 54
distribution, 10, 16, 19, 44, 55, 64, 83, 144
diversity, 10, 18, 84
dividends, 127, 128
Doha, 132
doors, 121
double counting, 65
download, 53
DuPont, 85

E

earnings, 53
earth, 5, 55, 56, 57, 59
ecological, 123, 125, 126
economic development, ix, 1, 6
economic growth, 123, 128, 129, 130, 131, 132
economic incentives, 84
economic systems, 130
economics, 53, 123
ecosystems, 79, 123
Education, 125
educational institutions, 20
Edwards Air Force Base, 141
electric power, vii, 3, 102
electric utilities, 94, 128
electricity, vii, viii, ix, 1, 2, 3, 4, 5, 6, 7, 9, 12, 13, 14, 15, 16, 17, 18, 19, 21, 22, 23, 25, 26, 27, 28, 29, 30, 36, 37, 39, 46, 48, 54, 55, 56, 57, 58, 59, 60, 62, 65, 66, 67, 68, 69, 70, 72, 73, 81, 82, 86, 88, 90, 109, 135, 139, 140, 141, 143, 144, 145
emission, viii, 3, 86, 104, 117, 129, 132

emitters, 132
employees, 4, 9, 20, 43, 44, 86, 87, 88, 91, 94, 139, 143, 144
employment, 126, 129
energy, vii, viii, ix, 1, 2, 3, 4, 5, 7, 8, 9, 10, 13, 14, 15, 18, 19, 20, 21, 22, 23, 24, 25, 26, 29, 30, 31, 33, 34, 35, 36, 38, 41, 42, 43, 44, 46, 47, 48, 49, 50, 51, 52, 53, 54, 55, 56, 57, 58, 59, 60, 61, 62, 63, 64, 65, 67, 70, 71, 72, 73, 74, 79, 80, 81, 82, 83, 84, 86, 88, 90, 94, 95, 103, 104, 106, 108, 113, 114, 119, 121, 125, 126, 127, 128, 129, 130, 131, 132, 134, 135, 136, 140, 141, 143
energy audit, 21
energy consumption, 21, 86
energy efficiency, viii, 4, 9, 21, 30, 35, 48, 53, 60, 62, 64, 70, 72, 79, 90, 103, 126, 131, 132, 134
Energy Efficiency and Renewable Energy, 53, 111
Energy Information Administration, 11
energy markets, viii, 4
energy supply, viii, 1, 18, 131, 140
engines, 7, 18, 89
enrollment, 66
enterprise, 78
environment, vii, ix, 1, 2, 3, 5, 7, 8, 26, 42, 45, 56, 62, 63, 64, 78, 86, 88, 89, 90, 91, 93, 100, 101, 102, 103, 105, 112, 114, 119, 121, 122, 126, 127, 134, 137, 140, 141
environmental audit, 90
environmental characteristics, 26, 74
environmental degradation, 94
environmental impact, vii, viii, 1, 2, 3, 5, 6, 7, 8, 14, 21, 26, 56, 57, 58, 64, 88, 89, 90, 98, 99, 104, 135, 139, 140, 143
environmental issues, 9, 87, 94, 97, 98, 117
environmental movement, 78, 87, 88, 89, 92
environmental policy, 89, 91, 92
environmental protection, 63, 94, 99, 114, 134

Index

Environmental Protection Agency (EPA), 2, 9, 21, 23, 43, 45, 47, 49, 50, 54, 57, 62, 63, 89, 92, 94, 128, 134, 139, 140, 141, 142, 143, 144
environmental regulations, 91
environmental standards, 28, 47, 122
environmental technology, 78, 86
environmentalists, 47, 112
equilibrium, 55
equity, 113, 114
estimating, 28
estimator, 53
ethane, 17
ethanol, 121
evening, 102
evening news, 102
Executive Order, 59, 60, 61, 62, 63, 64, 72, 73
expenditures, 94
expert, iv, 123, 140
expertise, 20, 23, 34, 39, 41, 66, 90, 98
extinction, 124

F

farmers, 9
farming, 99
fear, 102
February, 48, 49
Federal Energy Regulatory Commission, 51
federal government, 6, 31, 36, 59, 60, 61, 62, 63, 65, 68, 71, 73, 112, 139
federal law, 92
fee, 14, 33, 70
feeding, 124
fees, 40
feet, 17
fermentation, 85
fiber, 127
fibers, 61
finance, 36, 54
financial performance, 90
financing, 36, 38, 39, 52, 70, 92, 93
fire, 40, 90, 113, 127

firms, 113, 114, 117, 129
fish, 5, 26, 58, 99, 120
flexibility, 13, 15, 27, 29, 66, 100
flood, 5
flow, 53, 114
flow of capital, 114
fluctuations, 27
fluorescent light, 121
focusing, 86, 122
food, 28, 48, 82
Ford, 86
foreign direct investment, 131
forestry, 98, 132
forests, 57, 98, 103, 105
fossil, vii, 2, 3, 7, 8, 18, 21, 55, 56, 57, 90, 126, 129
fossil fuel, viii, 3, 7, 8, 21, 55, 56, 57, 90, 126, 129
fossil fuels, 21, 55, 56, 57
franchise, 55
fresh water, 113
friendship, 96
fruits, 98, 104
fuel, viii, 3, 5, 7, 8, 10, 17, 18, 22, 23, 25, 30, 35, 36, 40, 55, 83, 86, 87, 90, 99, 104, 114, 121, 126, 129
fuel cell, 5, 17, 36, 87, 114, 121
fuel-efficient vehicles, 86
funding, 36, 60, 70, 97
funds, 20, 70, 93, 114
furnaces, 82

G

Gallup, 92
Gallup Poll, 92
gas, vii, 3, 5, 7, 17, 18, 55, 56, 60, 67, 81, 82, 90, 95, 102, 128
gas turbine, 7, 17
gases, 55, 56, 57, 82
gasification, 79
gauge, 33, 62
GDP, 126, 128, 129
GE, 82, 83, 86
General Electric, 78, 82, 83, 86, 103, 135

General Motors, 84, 87, 90
General Services Administration, 61, 74
General Services Administration (GSA), 61
generation, vii, ix, 1, 2, 3, 4, 5, 7, 9, 13, 14, 15, 16, 17, 18, 19, 20, 22, 23, 25, 26, 27, 35, 36, 37, 38, 39, 40, 41, 46, 53, 54, 55, 56, 57, 58, 61, 62, 63, 67, 69, 82, 126, 132, 135
generators, 19, 33, 34, 51, 53, 82
Geneva, 84
Georgia, 123
geothermal, vii, 3, 5, 7, 26, 36, 52, 59, 61, 71, 82, 114, 140
geothermal systems, 82
Germany, 86, 132
gift, 46
global climate change, 7, 57
Global Reporting Initiative, 117
global trade, 99
global warming, 49, 56, 57, 79, 99, 136
globalization, 97
goals, viii, 3, 4, 8, 24, 29, 31, 42, 60, 61, 62, 63, 71, 73, 85, 89, 100, 103, 128, 140, 141, 142, 143
gold, 127
goods and services, 64, 65, 132
government, viii, 1, 3, 6, 23, 31, 34, 36, 38, 43, 46, 54, 59, 60, 61, 62, 63, 64, 65, 66, 68, 71, 73, 74, 77, 78, 82, 84, 87, 88, 89, 92, 97, 98, 99, 112, 113, 117, 123, 124, 125, 126, 127, 128, 130, 131, 134, 139
government intervention, 88
government policy, 78
government procurement, 73
grants, 97
grasses, 61
greed, 132
green energy, 82
green power, vii, viii, ix, x, 1, 2, 3, 4, 5, 6, 7, 8, 9, 10, 12, 13, 14, 15, 19, 20, 21, 22, 23, 24, 25, 26, 27, 28, 29, 30, 31, 32, 33, 36, 38, 42, 43, 44, 45, 46, 47, 48, 49, 55, 56, 57, 58, 59, 60, 62, 63, 65, 66, 67, 71, 72, 73, 74, 139, 140, 141, 142, 143, 144, 145
greenhouse, 8, 42, 43, 54, 55, 56, 57, 60, 62, 79, 83, 86, 90, 117, 123, 126, 128, 130, 131, 132, 136
greenhouse gas, 8, 42, 43, 54, 56, 57, 60, 62, 79, 83, 86, 90, 117, 123, 126, 128, 130, 131, 132, 136
greenhouse gases, 42, 56, 57, 79, 83, 86, 90, 123, 130
greening, 78
gross domestic product, 126
groundwater, 89
grouper, 51
groups, 24, 26, 39, 51, 87, 88, 91, 97, 113, 131, 136, 139
growth, 10, 44, 85, 87, 88, 91, 94, 112, 113, 119, 123, 128, 129, 130, 131, 132, 136
guidance, 61
guidelines, 33, 52, 70, 73, 92, 98, 117
guilt, 104

H

halogenated, 57
Harvard, 133
health, vii, 2, 7, 20, 24, 43, 57, 64, 94, 126
health care, 126
healthcare, 140
heat, 5, 17, 18, 21, 35, 55, 56, 62, 71, 88
heat pumps, 71
heating, 3, 5, 70, 101
heavy metal, 26
heavy metals, 26
height, 17
high-level, 20, 42, 91
hips, 82
holistic, 126
host, 38, 44
hotels, 104
households, 47, 128
housing, 125
human, vii, 2, 7, 42, 55, 56, 57, 64, 97, 99
human rights, 97

humanity, 123, 124
hybrid, 79, 127
hydro, vii, 7, 26, 52, 140
hydroelectric power, 58
hydrogen, 18, 87, 90, 121
hydropower, 3, 26, 58, 59

I

Idaho, 137
Illinois, 110
implementation, 22, 69
incentive, 31, 36, 37, 60
incentives, 6, 31, 35, 36, 37, 40, 42, 44, 51, 82, 89
income, 9, 53, 130
India, 130, 131
Indian, 71
indicators, 126, 134
indices, 114
indigenous, 10
industrial, vii, 3, 127, 130
industrialization, 94
industry, 9, 14, 18, 24, 38, 54, 55, 83, 86, 89, 90, 98, 99, 101, 103, 104, 105, 126, 128, 132, 135
infancy, 105
information exchange, 99
infrared, 57
infrastructure, 10, 130
initial public offerings, 114
injury, iv
innovation, 88, 140
in-state, 27
institutional reforms, 131
institutions, ix, 2, 20, 32, 72, 77, 97, 130, 131
insulation, 110
insurance, 35, 40
integration, 127
intellectual property, 130
intellectual property rights, 130
intelligence, 74
intensity, 60, 128, 130, 131
interactions, 45

Intergovernmental Panel on Climate Change, 123
internal combustion, 17, 18
internal rate of return, 53, 54
International Organization for Standardization, 90
International Organization for Standardization (ISO), 90
Internet, 27, 77, 82, 134
interval, 21, 57
intervention, 88
interview, 85, 86, 136
inventories, 54
investment, viii, 4, 18, 22, 34, 36, 38, 57, 82, 88, 92, 93, 114, 117, 119, 129, 130, 131
investors, 78, 87, 88, 91, 93, 112, 113, 114, 116, 117, 134, 136, 139, 144
isolation, 120

J

January, 9, 113, 117, 133, 135, 136
Japan, 130, 131
job creation, 49
jobs, 9, 94
judge, 29, 40, 113

K

Kyoto Protocol, 105

L

labeling, 48
labor, 119, 130
labor force, 130
land, 5, 17, 26, 37, 40, 71, 89
landfill, 5, 17, 18, 23, 35, 67
landfill gas, 23, 35, 67
landfills, 17
land-use, 37, 40
language, 65
large-scale, 98

law, 59, 130
laws, 19, 35, 51, 89, 91, 92
lead, 26, 29, 30, 45, 72, 79, 125, 126, 127, 129
leadership, 8, 9, 63, 123, 127, 135, 140, 141, 144
learning, 126
LED, 121
legislation, 122, 136
legislative, 129
legislative proposals, 129
licenses, 40
liens, 40
lifecycle, 105
life-cycle, 34, 90
life-cycle cost, 34
likelihood, 91
limitations, 24, 40, 67
links, 48, 49, 51
litigation, 89
living conditions, 127
lobbying, 92
lobbyists, 91
local community, 141
local government, viii, 3, 34
location, 13, 15, 34, 39, 69, 73
logging, 98
logistics, 83, 143
long-term, 10, 15, 67, 85, 129, 132, 141
Los Angeles, 86
losses, 112
lower prices, 67
loyalty, 143

M

machines, 119
magnetic, iv
Maine, 96
mainstream, 79, 102, 103, 117
maintenance, 38, 39, 40, 41, 64
management, viii, 4, 8, 12, 20, 21, 28, 42, 48, 60, 62, 73, 87, 88, 90, 92, 94, 101, 112, 113, 117, 119, 128, 142
management practices, 90, 142

mandates, 126
man-made, 79, 130
manufactured goods, 79
manufacturer, 38, 83, 119, 122, 140
manufacturing, 10, 18, 38, 45, 64, 79, 82, 83, 94
manure, 17
market, 6, 9, 12, 23, 25, 27, 31, 33, 47, 56, 58, 62, 63, 65, 66, 67, 68, 69, 74, 88, 89, 101, 103, 114, 127, 130, 131, 140, 141, 144
market prices, 67
market structure, 23
marketing, 5, 20, 42, 45, 46, 47, 78, 103
markets, vii, viii, ix, 1, 2, 3, 4, 6, 10, 22, 33, 34, 43, 46, 48, 49, 55, 56, 57, 64, 65, 67
Maryland, 49, 105
MAS, 67, 68
Massachusetts, 50
maximum price, 30
measurement, 106
measures, 35, 57, 80, 81, 89
media, 8, 44, 89, 103, 143
megawatt, 17, 58, 82
membership, 97
merchandise, 46
mercury, 43, 134
messages, 72
methane, 5, 17, 18, 36, 55, 57, 67, 82
metric, 43
Microsoft, 86
Millennium, 123
mining, 94
misconceptions, 28
missions, 7, 95, 129, 130, 140
models, 54
modules, 17, 35
money, 12, 29, 40, 56, 78, 80, 114, 119, 120, 126, 133
monopoly, 55
Monroe, 128
morale, 9, 43
moratorium, 127
motivation, 9, 85, 91

Index

movement, 79
municipal solid waste, 26, 59
mutual funds, 114

N

nation, vii, 3, 9, 10, 47, 48, 63, 70, 73, 90
national, viii, 4, 6, 15, 18, 19, 23, 44, 63, 74, 88, 105, 108, 116, 126, 131, 132, 136, 143
National Public Radio, 136
national security, viii, 4, 6, 18, 63
Native American, 71
Native Americans, 71
natural, vii, 3, 5, 18, 55, 56, 57, 80, 81, 90, 95, 101, 107, 108, 109, 120
natural capital, 120
natural gas, vii, 3, 18, 56, 81, 90, 95
natural resources, 80
negotiation, 32
net metering, 16
network, 97
New Jersey, 33, 42
New York, iii, iv, 51, 83, 101, 106, 111, 115, 133
New York Stock Exchange, 111
newsletters, 44
niche market, 10
Nike, 103
nitrogen, 43, 104
nitrogen oxides, 43
nitrous oxide, 57, 89
nongovernmental, 65, 96
nongovernmental organization, 65, 96
non-profit, 6
non-tariff barriers, 132
nontoxic, 108
normal, 8, 66, 113
North America, 81
North Carolina, 52, 107
Northeast, 43
nuclear, vii, 2, 3, 56, 90, 95, 121, 126
nuclear power, 95
nuclear power plant, 95

O

obligation, 63
Ohio, 93
oil, vii, 3, 56, 90, 95, 121
oils, 127
Oklahoma, 113
online, 21, 54, 58, 79, 123, 134, 135, 136
Oregon, 36, 95
organic, 5, 48, 61
organic food, 48
organic matter, 61
organization, ix, 2, 4, 8, 12, 13, 19, 20, 21, 22, 23, 25, 27, 28, 29, 30, 31, 32, 33, 34, 35, 36, 37, 38, 39, 40, 41, 42, 44, 45, 57, 90, 98, 120, 134, 139, 140, 141, 142, 143, 144
organizations, vii, viii, ix, 1, 2, 3, 4, 6, 9, 10, 12, 13, 14, 15, 16, 20, 21, 23, 27, 28, 30, 31, 38, 43, 45, 46, 47, 65, 78, 92, 96, 97, 98, 103, 112, 135, 139, 141, 142, 143, 144
oxide, 57
ozone, 57, 104

P

Pacific, 113, 130, 132
packaging, 9, 64, 78, 99
paper, 117, 127
parabolic, 71
partnership, 54, 72, 92, 99, 100, 104, 144
partnerships, 46, 92, 96, 98, 99, 103
passenger, 139
passive, 5, 70
patents, 134
peak demand, 21
Pennsylvania, 30, 33, 51, 107, 109, 141
pension, 93
per capita, 90, 132
perceptions, 28
performance, 8, 17, 22, 38, 41, 48, 79, 86, 89, 90, 91, 92, 93, 94, 114, 136, 143
performance indicator, 48

periodic, 41
permit, 57, 60, 92
personal, 101, 126
personal relevance, 126
PFC, 90
photographs, 77
photovoltaic, 5, 17, 42, 45, 52, 102
photovoltaic cells, 17, 102
photovoltaics, 51, 53
planetary, 124
planning, 20, 31, 32, 113
plants, 17, 26, 61, 90, 107, 113, 127
platinum, 108, 109
play, 85, 112
policy instruments, 89
policy makers, 88, 89, 91, 94, 128, 129, 132
policy making, 91
policymakers, 129
political stability, 136
pollutant, 89
pollutants, 42, 89
pollution, vii, 3, 18, 84, 87, 89, 90, 92, 94, 95, 97, 102, 104, 113, 117, 126, 127
pond, 100, 106
poor, 94, 127
population, 124, 126, 130, 132
portfolio, viii, 4, 7, 21, 26, 59, 81, 112
portfolios, 104
potato, 82
potential energy, 131
poverty, 127
power, vii, viii, ix, x, 1, 2, 3, 4, 5, 6, 7, 8, 9, 10, 12, 13, 14, 15, 16, 17, 18, 19, 20, 21, 22, 23, 24, 25, 26, 27, 28, 29, 30, 31, 32, 33, 34, 35, 36, 37, 38, 39, 40, 41, 42, 43, 44, 45, 46, 47, 48, 49, 53, 54, 55, 56, 57, 58, 59, 60, 61, 62, 63, 65, 66, 67, 68, 69, 71, 72, 73, 74, 80, 81, 82, 88, 89, 90, 95, 98, 102, 103, 113, 114, 121, 126, 132, 139, 140, 141, 142, 143, 144, 145
power generation, vii, 2, 7, 13, 16, 17, 55, 58, 63, 82, 126, 132
power outage, 7, 35

power plant, 18, 54, 89, 90, 113, 114
power plants, 18, 89, 90, 95, 113, 114
powers, 45
PPA, 39
precipitation, 57
preference, 64
premium, 12, 13, 14, 36, 57, 59, 72
premiums, 12, 16
preparedness, 112
president, 20, 98, 123, 135, 136
pressure, 94, 98
prevention, 87, 90, 92, 95, 117
price instability, 7
price stability, 27, 141, 143
prices, 7, 10, 25, 27, 36, 37, 67, 70, 90, 126, 129
priorities, 99
private, 92, 103, 113, 114, 130
private-sector, 130
proactive, 122
production, 9, 10, 17, 35, 41, 52, 64, 90, 94, 99
production costs, 10
productivity, 9, 127, 129, 130
productivity growth, 130
profit, 6, 134
profits, 78, 79, 83, 94, 98, 119, 133, 136
program, 6, 8, 9, 12, 25, 30, 37, 43, 44, 47, 48, 51, 66, 69, 72, 74, 80, 82, 83, 96, 104, 120, 124, 132, 134, 139
promote, 44, 45, 64, 112, 123
property, iv, 36, 37, 130
propulsion, 84
prosperity, 102, 134
protection, 16, 47, 58, 63, 94, 99, 114, 117, 134
prototype, 81, 107
proxy, 117
public, viii, 4, 8, 14, 15, 23, 28, 32, 42, 43, 44, 45, 47, 65, 79, 80, 88, 91, 92, 93, 94, 96, 103, 111, 114, 127, 136, 143
public education, 47
public goods, 88
public markets, 65
public opinion, 80

Index

public policy, 79
public relations, viii, 4, 8, 42, 44, 143
public sector, 127
public support, 94
publishers, 77
pumps, 71
purchasing power, 25
pure water, 87

Q

qualifications, 32, 39, 40
quality of life, 93, 94, 127

R

R and D, 54, 75, 82, 128, 129
race, 124
radiation, 57
rain, 89
rainwater, 100, 107
range, viii, 3, 4, 17, 25, 46, 56, 73, 86, 90, 97
rate of return, 34, 42
ratings, 24
raw material, 64, 119
raw materials, 64, 119
reading, 61
real estate, 81, 103
real-time basis, 16
rebates, 36
recession, 129
recognition, 8, 19, 43, 44, 92, 105, 130, 140, 142, 144
reconcile, 130
recycling, 103
reduction, 8, 22, 31, 33, 43, 62, 67, 68, 81, 84, 86, 98, 99, 104, 109, 117, 128, 132
redundancy, 18
Reform Act, 66
reforms, 131
refrigeration, 101, 121
regenerate, 102
regional, 7, 40, 99, 131
registries, 54
Registry, 43, 54
regular, 14
regulation, 7, 91
regulations, x, 2, 7, 60, 68, 69, 89, 91, 92, 98, 112, 123, 125
regulators, 8
regulatory bodies, 116
relationship, 96, 129, 131
relevance, 126
reliability, 16, 18, 22, 28, 38
remediation, 112
renewable energy, vii, viii, ix, 1, 2, 3, 4, 5, 6, 7, 8, 9, 10, 13, 14, 16, 17, 22, 23, 25, 26, 27, 28, 30, 33, 34, 36, 37, 38, 44, 45, 46, 47, 48, 49, 52, 53, 54, 55, 56, 57, 58, 59, 60, 61, 62, 63, 64, 65, 66, 67, 69, 70, 71, 72, 73, 75, 82, 90, 93, 104, 105, 121, 135, 140
renewable resource, vii, ix, 1, 2, 3, 5, 9, 10, 14, 15, 16, 18, 25, 34, 35, 37, 56, 57, 58, 59, 61, 65, 69, 70, 140
reputation, 24
research, viii, 23, 24, 25, 45, 79, 82, 83, 92, 112, 114, 128, 130, 131, 136
research and development, 51, 61, 82, 92, 128
reservoir, 58
residential, 53, 85, 127
residues, 61
resistance, 28
resolution, 117
resources, vii, ix, 1, 2, 3, 5, 6, 7, 9, 10, 13, 14, 15, 16, 18, 21, 23, 25, 26, 27, 34, 35, 37, 41, 47, 48, 50, 51, 55, 56, 57, 58, 59, 61, 63, 65, 67, 69, 73, 74, 80, 98, 99, 102, 103, 119, 121, 124, 140, 142
responsibilities, 63
responsiveness, 8, 63
restaurants, 48
restructuring, 13, 48, 68
retail, 23, 24, 33, 39, 46, 49, 55, 57, 58, 66, 68, 81, 113, 140
retention, 60

returns, 38
risk, 7, 10, 16, 22, 29, 38, 57, 68, 112, 113, 124, 139
risk management, 113
risks, ix, 1, 7, 65, 93, 112, 114, 123, 143
rivers, 97
robustness, 10
rule of law, 130
rural, 9
rural communities, 9
Russian, 77

S

SA, 67
safeguards, 47
safety, 20, 40, 86, 94, 126
sales, 36, 45, 83, 113
sample, 12, 33, 49
savings, 22, 30, 38, 52, 60, 72, 80, 81, 122, 131, 141
school, 17, 110
scientific community, 79
scientists, 56
sea level, 57
search, 25, 68, 82
security, viii, ix, 1, 4, 6, 18, 63, 75, 140
selecting, 20, 24, 70
series, 113, 132
service provider, 36, 67
services, iv, 7, 9, 21, 30, 38, 39, 55, 64, 65, 67, 70, 74, 92, 127, 132
sewage, 17
shape, 35
shaping, 91
shareholders, 8, 86, 93, 139
shares, 114
shingles, 17
short period, 5
shortage, 113
short-term, 27, 29
shy, 112, 116
sign, 13, 46, 66, 115
signals, 126, 127
signs, 27, 94

silicon, 82, 122
sites, x, 2, 6, 24, 39, 44, 73, 74, 77, 92, 104, 112
sludge, 102
smoke, 102
software, 35, 53, 86
soil, 110
solar, vii, 3, 5, 7, 13, 23, 26, 36, 38, 39, 42, 52, 53, 57, 59, 61, 70, 71, 81, 82, 83, 88, 95, 102, 106, 114, 121, 140
solar cell, 114
solar collectors, 71
solar energy, 5, 7, 83
solar panels, 81, 83, 88, 106
solar system, 70
solid waste, 26, 59
solutions, 22, 48, 49, 50, 79, 86, 89, 92, 95, 114, 124
South Carolina, 18
South Korea, 130
species, 124
speed, 87
spelling, 89, 102
spills, 92
sponsor, 144
stability, 8, 27, 136, 141, 143
stabilize, 123
stages, 20
stakeholder, 6, 139
stakeholder groups, 139
stakeholders, ix, 1, 12, 14, 44, 71, 86, 88, 91, 131, 141, 143, 144
standards, 14, 19, 28, 38, 43, 47, 51, 78, 79, 105, 122, 127, 142
statutes, 92
statutory, 60
steel, 79, 119
stock, 117, 126
stock exchange, 117
storage, 7, 35, 40, 127
strategic, viii, 4, 45, 48, 99, 139
strategies, 12, 29, 42, 44, 46, 67, 70, 74, 87, 123
strength, 24
strokes, 127

Index

students, 20, 103, 110, 117, 124
subsidies, 12, 42, 126
subsidization, 68
sulfur, 43, 89
sulfur dioxide, 43, 89
summer, 110
Superfund, 112, 116
suppliers, 14, 16, 24, 27, 28, 30, 32, 33, 45, 46, 55, 56, 57, 66, 72, 73, 83, 99, 127
supply, 7, 14, 22, 26, 67, 79, 83, 90, 119, 120, 121, 141
supply chain, 79, 83, 90, 119, 120, 121
supply disruption, 7
sustainability, 85, 93, 117, 119, 120, 121, 122, 123, 126, 127, 134
sustainable development, 94, 126, 135
sustainable growth, 85, 87, 88
switching, 30, 55, 63, 142, 143
systems, 5, 10, 15, 17, 35, 36, 37, 38, 39, 40, 41, 42, 52, 55, 56, 60, 70, 71, 82, 88, 94, 125

T

tangible, 27
targets, 8, 117
tariff, 132
tax base, 9
tax credit, 36, 129
tax system, 126
taxes, 36, 126
teacher training, 126
technical assistance, 36, 70, 74
technological change, 130
technology, 17, 35, 37, 55, 70, 78, 79, 81, 82, 84, 86, 96, 106, 126, 130, 131, 132, 134
technology transfer, 130, 131
television, 103
temperature, 57, 113
territory, 25, 69
Texas, 8, 9, 100, 113, 136
The Economist, 112
thermal load, 18

thinking, 79, 104, 112, 113, 120
third party, 27
threats, 96, 124
thresholds, 67
time, vii, 3, 5, 8, 12, 13, 16, 22, 25, 32, 34, 35, 36, 37, 40, 41, 44, 56, 58, 78, 79, 86, 94, 96, 102, 104, 119, 136, 142, 143
title, 33, 136
tourism, 104
toxic, 94, 103, 112
toxins, 26
trade, 39, 48, 52, 84, 99, 123, 129, 132, 139
trading, 89, 99, 121
trading partners, 99
training, 40, 70, 74, 94, 126
transaction costs, 12, 38
transactions, ix, 2, 15
transfer, 130, 131, 132
transformation, 10, 63, 119
transmission, 16, 40, 55
transparency, 98
transportation, 3, 7, 83, 104, 132
travel, 104
trees, 61, 102
trend, 78, 79, 95, 104
trial, 29
tribal, 71
trucks, 83, 84, 121
trust, 100
turbulence, 17
turnover, 9, 94

U

U.S. economy, 94, 129
UK, 133
uncertainty, 59
unemployment, 128
unions, 94
United Nations, 124, 126
United Nations Environment Program, 124
United States, vii, 2, 3, 4, 10, 46, 48, 56, 59, 74, 77, 78, 82, 84, 87, 89, 90, 96,

98, 99, 103, 112, 117, 121, 122, 128, 129, 130, 131, 132, 135, 136
universe, 114
universities, viii, 1, 3, 139

V

validation, 41
values, 25, 77, 126
vapor, 57
variable, 25, 57, 67
vegetation, 110
vehicles, 71, 84, 86, 127
ventilation, 101
Vermont, 106
Vice President, 91
visible, 16, 32
vision, 127, 135
volatility, 16, 39, 141, 143
voters, 92
voting, 92
vulnerability, 10

W

Wall Street Journal, 135
War on Terror, 125
waste products, 18
wastes, 61
water, 5, 9, 57, 58, 60, 64, 70, 87, 89, 96, 97, 99, 104, 122
water quality, 58
water resources, 57, 99
water vapor, 57
watershed, 58
wealth, 126
well-being, 94, 126
wholesale, 33, 49
wildlife, 54, 57
wind, vii, 3, 5, 9, 10, 13, 17, 18, 22, 23, 26, 27, 33, 35, 51, 53, 59, 61, 82, 90, 95, 105, 106, 114, 121, 140
wind farm, 27, 105, 114
wind speeds, 17
wind turbines, 5, 17, 82, 95
windows, 108
wine, 48
winning, 9, 136
winter, 110
Wisconsin, 43, 54, 82
wood, 61, 102, 117
wood waste, 61
workers, 94
World Bank, 130
World Business Council for Sustainable Development, 99, 134, 135
World Resources Institute, ix, 2, 33, 46, 49, 50, 54
World Resources Institute (WRI), ix, 2
writing, 33, 41, 101

Z

zoning, 17, 40